CARLISLE BREWE
AND
PUBLIC HOUSI
1894 - 1916

BY
STEVEN DAVIDSON

Above, forgotten advertising from Carlisle's late Victorian/Edwardian licensing trade. However this curious character would have been well enough known to some of the city's drinkers of the period who frequented those public houses that were either owned or managed by the local wine and spirit merchants T & J Minns. The design was described in advertising of the time as meant to represent Bacchus. It can be found embossed on all their beer (from circa 1898) bottles and printed onto many spirit labels. It was also used as a decorative feature on at least one of the public houses that they were associated with as it is known to have been applied to the sheets of glass on the entrance doors at the original Apple Tree in Lowther Street.

PICTURE CREDITS
AEROFILMS, page 13.
ALAN MAIR, page 34,57,67.
ANDREW CUNNINGHAM, page 25, top
ASHLEY KENDAL, pages 49,77,79,90, rear cover top.
AUTHOR, pages 1,9,19,20 top, 26,33,36 bottom, 39 ,41,58,61,62 bottom, 65,70,74,78,80,92,104,120,121 bottom, 131 right, 132 right, 134,135,136,137,138,139,141.
BILL BOAK, pages 15,88.
CARLISLE LIBRARY, page 8 bottom, 18,20,37,38,42,43,44,45,48,50,55,56,62 top,64 top,68,69,72,73,82,86,89,91,94,100,101, 102,103,106,110,111,114,115,116,122.
CHARLES FARTHING page 130.
CN GROUP LIMITED, page 35 top, 83,95,112,117.
CUMBRIA RECORD OFFICE, pages 4,10,11,27,36 top,40,52,53,59,63 top, 64 bottom, 69 top, 75,99,107, 119,128, rear cover bottom.
DAVID HAY, page 21top.
DENIS PERRIAM, page 16 bottom, 118, 121top.
JIM TEMPLETON, page 54.
JOHN MINNS, pages 84,85,123,125.
JOHN PARKER, page76.
LEWIS OSWALD, page 108
MARGARET HODGSON, page 16 top, 18 top, 63 bottom.
MIKE DICKINSON, front cover top left and pages 51, 140.
PAT HONEYMAN, pages 60,71,109.
PAUL THEAKSTON, page 8 Top
SCOTTISH BREWING ARCHIVE, pages 6,24,131,132
TULLIE HOUSE MUSEUM and ART GALLERY, pages 7,25 bottom, 28,29,47,66 top, 93,113.

ACKNOWLEDGEMENTS:
The staff at Carlisle Record Office who have been most helpful during the course of research for this book, Stephen White at Carlisle Library, Matthew Constantine at Tullie House, Ian Caruana for information on tokens, Margaret Hodgson, Alan Mair of the City Planning Department, Bill Boak, Ashley Kendal, Pat Honeyman, Norman Nicholson, Mike Dickinson for pub flasks, Andrew Cunningham, Michael Jones and Norman Barber of the Brewery History Society, Paul Theakston Black Sheep Brewery Masham, Hugh Curley Head Brewer at the Carlisle Old Brewery during the Theakston years, Dr Keith Thomas BREWLAB, Dennis.R.Dickins of Cumbria Environmental and Geological Services, John Ingram Hydrogeologist at the Enviroment Agency, Alma Topen at the Scottish Brewery Archive, Jeff Davidson for stone bottle photos and artwork on pages 20 and 61and finally special thanks must go to Carlisle Historian Denis Perriam who has kindly provided me with a wealth of references from his own extensive studies into the Carlisle Journal newspapers.

BIBLIOGRAPHY:
A HISTORY OF BREWING by H.S. CORRAN David & Charles publishers 1975.
THE BREWER A Familiar Treatise on the Art Of Brewing by W.R. LOFTUS London 1874/75.
VICTORIAN PUBLIC HOUSES by BRIAN SPILLER David & Charles publishers 1972.

NEWSPAPERS, CUMBERLAND PACQUET 1781 - 1802, CARLISLE JOURNAL 1802 - 1827, 1890 - 1900.

CARLISLE TRADE/STREET DIRECTORIES, 1828 - 1913

MAPS, WOOD'S 1821, STUDHOLME'S 1842, 1846/48, ASQUITH'S 1853 and the ORDNANCE SURVEYS of 1865 and 1899.

CARLISLE BUILDING INSPECTORS PLANS, deposited in the record office.

LICENSING REGISTER BOOKS, 1822 - 26, 1872, 1875, 1887 and 1894 all deposited at the record office.

MARYPORT BREWERY SALES/STOCK LEDGERS 1911 deposited at the record office.

British Library Cataloguing In Publication Data
A catalogue record for this book is available from the British Library ISBN 0 9547739 0 X

Published by: P3 Publications	**Printed by:** Amadeus Press
13 Beaver Road	West 26 Business Park
Carlisle	Cleckheaton
Cumbria, CA2 7PS	BD19 4TQ

INTRODUCTION

An interest in collecting Carlisle Victorian bottles, which has spanned some 25 years, has provided the incentive to research and compile this book, the names and trade marks embossed or printed onto them are often from long gone Carlisle breweries and pubs .The bottles then, are in a way the spark to a wider study of the City's drink trade during the late Victorian era.

This is for the first time in print a review of Carlisle's Victorian breweries pre State Management. This is not surprising as during the course of my research it has been disappointing to find such a lack of detailed records, plans, photos etc, it is likely that the sudden closure of the breweries at what was quite an early date to have been the main cause for this scarcity of records. Nevertheless, some information regarding what was an interesting and forgotten branch of Carlisle Victorian industry has been uncovered.

Regarding the Carlisle public houses we get onto a better footing for written detail and are lucky to have a good photographic record. The book is based around a set of thirty-one photographs, which depict Carlisle licensed premises about*1901/02 (The original glass plate negatives for these still exist and are in the possession of Tullie House Museum and Art Gallery). Many have appeared in print before, but this is the first time they have been drawn together into one publication. They were taken by or for John Minns. In 1905 he was the owner of the Wellington in English Street (now the site of Yates) and managed four other properties the principal of these being the 'Gaol Tap', which was the largest and most impressive public house at that time. The reason why he had these pub photos taken is, unfortunately, not known but without them this book would have been impossible to put together. These views have been supplemented with further selected pictures and photos and as a result a total of 60 of Carlisle's 117 public houses in 1894 are illustrated, and a known history of each of these properties is given.

The start date of this book, 1894, was chosen for a number of reasons 1. a licensed register of that date exists at Carlisle Records Office listing all properties from massive hotels down to corner grocers' shops. 2. a reasonable number of the pubs that stood in Carlisle at this late Victorian period can be shown by either using photos taken around the same time or more recent 20th century views. However, if a study of the city's pre-1894 public houses had been attempted then it would have resulted with many more properties which could not be viewed with a print or photograph. At least 30 pubs were either demolished or closed in the years between 1840-93 and none of these can be illustrated.

The cut - off date for the book is the arrival of the State Management scheme (1916-1971), the passing of which is still talked about with some regret, but this subject has had some attention in recent years and, in a way, it has overshadowed the earlier history of Carlisle's breweries and public houses.

Finally, in the event of any reader having information or original Victorian/ Edwardian records, plans, maps, prints, photos, advertising, or old labels relating to Carlisle's breweries and public houses pre-1916, i.e. before the Central Liquor Traffic/State Management take over, then I would very much like to see and hopefully get a copy of such material as the information contained in this book is very likely only part of the detail known about this subject. I am also interested in tracing the original photograph of workers in the Old Brewery yard, see page 8. I can be contacted at the address given below.

STEVEN DAVIDSON,
208, DALSTON ROAD,
CARLISLE,
CUMBRIA,
CA2 6DY.

* Note five of these photos namely the Waggon and Horses, Samson, Ordnance Arms, Drove and the Light Horseman seem to have been taken slightly earlier than others from the Minns collection. These earlier dates are pointed out when these particular pubs are reviewed in the book.

CARLISLE BREWERIES
IN 1894

During the course of research for this book a number of Victorian brewing papers, namely *The Brewing Trade Review* and *The Brewers Guardian* have been consulted. Dating from the 1870's to 1916 these failed to carry any reference to the Carlisle breweries. During the late 1880's a certain Alfred Barnard visited 111 breweries and published his findings in four volumes between 1889 -1891, entitled *Noted Breweries of Great Britain & Ireland*, but there were no visits to the Carlisle breweries by him.

Considering the above, it would seem that Carlisle was not well-known or of much importance as a brewing town during the 19th century. However, a statement in *Bulmers Directory for Cumberland ,1901*, conflicts with that conclusion. It states in a brief reference to Carlisle breweries, 'one of the first things to strike a Carlisle man on landing in Australia will be the sign of FINE CARLISLE ALE SOLD HERE.'

There were of course other British breweries sending export ale to Australia at this time. Principal amongst these were the Edinburgh breweries of Youngers and McEwans, but the Carlisle beer must have been in demand and carried some reputation considering some of the quality beers it was having to compete with. Bulmers Directory also states that there was more than one Carlisle brewery doing an export trade to the colonies, but it fails to name them. Some years earlier though, an entry in the *Carlisle Journal* newspaper for the 30 July 1880 does name a brewery. It printed the following which appeared in the *Australian Trade Review* of the 10 June 1880; 'Some very fine shipments have lately been landed of the Carlisle New Brewery Co's *brand in half Hogsheads and Kilderkins'. Three years later we get further information about this brewery's trade to Australia which gives us the exact destination for the Carlisle beer as the Carlisle Journal on the 16 February 1883 reported that an article about the New Brewery's beers had appeared in the *Melbourne Argus* for January of that year. Unfortunately this turns out to have been a small advert which reads 'New Brewery, Carlisle Ale- now landing ex Gulf of St Vincent steamer. Thomas Tyson Elizabeth St.'. Interestingly it seems this Carlisle brewery's export beer was said at the time to be more expensive than Bass and McEwans.

Returning to the Bulmers Directory comment which suggests there were other Carlisle breweries exporting beer, the 1884 advert below shows that the New Brewery's nearby rival was also involved in this trade though whether they were still exporting in 1901 is not known. This advert suggests that the destination of the Old Brewery's beer was not Australia, but to the Indian sub-continent, the market here being in the main (at this date) to the troops in the British army, although it should be pointed out that this brewery would have been only one of many other British firms sending their beer to this destination, as in 1884, 39,314 barrels of beer was exported to the Indian continent.

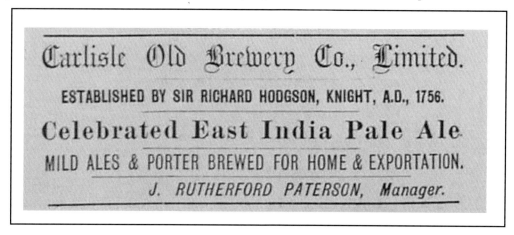

The main beer type exported by British Victorian breweries, as is the evidence for the Carlisle firms, was Pale Ale. This beer with its high hop levels, quite high alcohol content (by present day standards) and being brewed with hard water, all contributed to the beer's keeping properties which of course was essential considering the distances it had to travel and the hot climates it was being retailed in.

However, back in Carlisle, India Pale Ale/Bitter does not seem to have been in such demand judging by later local brewery records, the city's drinkers in the main preferring Mild Ale.

Here is a list of all the Carlisle breweries in 1894, Carlisle Old Brewery, Caldewgate; Carlisle New Brewery, Shaddongate, Established 1774; Graham's, Queens Head Brewery, Established 1860; Iredale's High Brewery ,Currock Street Established 1875/76 and Halls Crown Brewery, off Collier Lane Established 1869.

*Note, we know the beer type exported by this brewery to have been Pale Ale (Carlisle Journal 27 June 1890).

BREWERY WATER SUPPLIES

This subject is considered here separately as there is some surviving detail on all five of the Carlisle brewery water supplies and it is the obvious starting point for the whole brewing process. Besides the water used for turning into beer, it was also needed for cooling and washing purposes and for the breweries steam engine boiler.

Brewing water can be obtained from a town or city water supply, however, in the 19th century brewers more often drew their water from an on -site well, and this was the practice at the Carlisle breweries.

It is an industry that requires an abundant, reliable and pure supply of water if this could be secured on-site from either a well or a bore- hole, then there would be no need to resort to paying the local water company for the use of their supply.

Also during the 19th and early 20th century (before the widespread adoption by British breweries of cooling/ice making machinery) there was the importance of the temperature of a breweries well water in regards to its suitability for cooling requirements needed for when brewing during the summer months. If the breweries well water could be relied upon to provide sufficient and cold enough water at this time of the year (and in this latter respect this was more often the case than not) then this was of great value as the local town/city water works supply during this season would almost certainly have been of no use at all on account of its water temperature being too warm, and this was the situation with Carlisle's city supply as it is known not to have been cold enough during the summer.

The Carlisle Old Brewery sourced its brewing water from a 14 ft. deep well, said to have been the original sunk in 1756. The Carlisle New Brewery well was only 11ft., this was sunk in 1774. T. Grahams Queens Brewery, situated near the Joiners Arms in Caldewgate had their well at 14 foot depth. The depths of the well at Iredales is not known .Halls Crown Street Brewery seems to have had two water sources, one from a well and the other extracted from a machine drilled bore hole which was said to be deep.

It is surprising to find just how shallow the Caldewgate brewery wells were and this could have made them vulnerable to pollution. The brewing journals and books of the Victorian period urged brewers to sink their wells at least 25 feet deep to 'avoid organic impurities' and 'pollution from surface drainage'. Despite these directions there is evidence that the Caldewgate brewery wells were in good condition as T.Graham had the well water of his brewery sent for analysis in 1911 being concerned that it had recently become contaminated, however it was certified free from organic impurities. Also when the State Management took over the city's breweries in 1916 it seems they were intending to use the wells at the Old and New brewery sites and commented on their 'suitable purity' . Even so T. Graham switched to using the city mains supply in 1911 because of the above mentioned pollution scare. His well water, though now not used specifically for brewing with would, however, have likely been retained for other brewery purposes including its cooling advantages in summer.

Turning now to the actual chemistry of the water i.e. the natural minerals or salts present in the well supply, this became of some interest to the mid /late Victorian brewers as, put simply, if the water is 'Hard' then it is suited to brewing Pale Ales/Bitters, also a 'Hard' water contributes to the keeping qualities of the beer. If the water is 'Soft' or contains a fair amount of the carbonates of lime and magnesia then it is more suited to the darker beers like Mild and Stout .

From a 1911 letter referring to Grahams Queens Brewery well supply we are given detail based on a analysis that the water carried substantial levels of Sulphates, so we can say this water could be classed as 'Hard'. Just 2- 300 yards away though the other Caldewgate breweries, Carlisle Old/New were using well waters that, according to a State Management report dated 1916, were '*very suitable for brewing Mild Ale and Stout.*'

So it looks like there was totally different water at Graham's Queens brewery when compared to the Carlisle Old and New Breweries yet there was only some 2-300 yards between them and all breweries were sourcing their water at or near the same depth. After seeking expert advice to solve this it seems the answer lies with the influence of the River Caldew. The Carlisle Old Brewery lay immediately adjacent to it, the Carlisle New Brewery was about 60 - 80 yards from the said river. Apparently when water was being raised from both of these wells there would have been a draw-in effect pulling in river water (which is relatively 'Soft') through the gravel deposits which these wells were sunk in, in fact depending on the length of time of drawing on the well at the Old Brewery a considerable amount of the water would eventually end up being from the river. This mixing effect would also have had (though to a lesser extent) some influence on the New Brewery's Shaddongate well.

Grahams Queens Brewery, however was furthest away from the river and apparently it would have had little to no effect on the water sourced from this site.

BREWERY WATER SUPPLIES

The Victorian brewing books and journals generally considered 'Hard' water to be most suitable for brewing, but to the Carlisle breweries using a 'Soft' water supply this was no great problem as the natural water could be artificially hardened by adding gypsum salts when needed for brewing Pale Ales. In 1887 a J. Robinson & Co of Cotehill, advertised that they could supply 'clarifying gypsum for brewers use'.

Returning to the subject of a brewery's well water temperature during the summer season, further information on this point can be gleaned from records relating to Iredales Brewery which was situated behind the 'Cumberland Wrestlers' on the Currock Road.

In 1879 Jos.Iredale the owner and head brewer was considering selling his newly- built brewery and public houses to G.Wadley who had been the head brewer at the City of London Brewery. In a letter dated 23.10.1879 Wadley asks 'is there a good well of pure water, cold throughout the Summer? Copy of analysis of water, if you have it.' In reply Iredale said about his water supply 'there is an excellent, and I believe inexhaustible, well on the premises. I have raised as much as 500 barrels a day, it stands about 49 to 51 degrees Fahrenheit Winter and Summer, I enclose copies of two analyses'. Wadley in his reply referring to the above said 'I note there is a supply of excellent brewing water.'

The process of fermenting beer generates heat and during the summer months bulk brewing of beer under warm climatic conditions if not checked by adequate cooling is more liable to bacterial infection and 'frets' turning the beer sour or rendering unpleasant flavours when tasted. So the *main need for the cold water during the summer was to cool the fermenting beers in the fermentation vessels by running the cold well water through coiled tinned-copper pipes known as Attemperators (e.g. arrowed in illustration below) .This type of brewery fitting came widely into use during the 1840's.

However despite the introduction of Attemperators and Horizontal Refrigerators it seems some Victorian breweries still had difficulties with summer brewing. The reasons for this could be that the well did not yield a sufficient amount of water for cooling purposes, this situation could arise due to a combination of the summer season and other local factories drawing on the same ground water source as the breweries, causing the well to run short or even give-out at this time of year, this event was more likely to occur if the brewery happened to be located in a large industrial town/city. Alternatively the ground water may not have been cold enough, this could have been caused by the brewery drawing water up from a considerable depth (all of this then explains Wadleys question to Iredale on this point).

Those breweries that had these problems tended to brew from the months of October into April but this practice entailed the carrying of large stocks of beer for use in the summer. The introduction of cooling/ice making machinery from around 1870 was an important development in ending this seasonal problem, as this machinery could be used to chill down mains, river or even some well waters that otherwise would have been of a temperature unsuitable to brewery cooling requirements. However in these early years it was only some of the major British breweries that fitted this type of plant as the cost of such machinery was at this time prohibitive to it being acquired by the smaller firms.

From the information contained in the above letter Iredale's Carlisle brewery would seem to have had no difficulties with summer brewing as the well there yielded water at around 50°F which was an ideal temperature for cooling purposes, to underline this point the *Brewers Guardian* had this to say in an article in their paper of 23.7.1889. 'Where an unlimited supply of well water at 50-54°F can be obtained a cooling machine becomes of a minor importance for the summer production of sound beers' the same article also comments about the unsuitability of water sourced from a city or town reservoir supply, (Carlisle's Victorian water supply stood about 62°F during the summer) it goes on to say, 'During the five summer months the town's water usually rises to from 60-68°F, it is impossible with this to control the fermentations in the tuns or squares with water of such high temperatures running through the attemperators'. This last paragraph highlights the asset that a suitable well water supply could be to a Victorian/ Edwardian brewery.

*An abundant supply of cold water would also be required for running thru the Refrigerator to cool the wort (see p24).

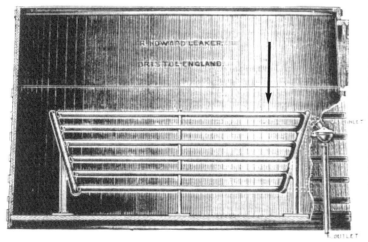

Section through a shallow round wooden fermenting vessel, or in brewing terms known as a Tun .The pipe work of the attemperator is arrowed. Round fermenting vessels are not known to have been fitted in Carlisle's Victorian breweries but because of the lack of records on the cities firms it shouldn't be ruled out. This illustration is taken from a brewery fittings catalogue which dates to 1904.

CARLISLE OLD BREWERY

Above: The Carlisle Old Brewery in 1971, which was its last year under State ownership.

The brewery was established in 1756 but there is some uncertainty that this date refers to the above location, all that can be definitely said at present about the early origins of the brewery is that it has been on the above Caldewgate site from at least 1791 as it is marked on Hutchinson's map of Carlisle at that date.

Despite the 18th century history of the brewery on the above site, the buildings seen in this photo are of no great age as the top two storeys and 'saw edge' roof structures with louvered ventilators can be dated to 1894 (see plans on page 10) being built up off brickwork of an earlier and what seems to have been a lower elevation building that was built along the rivers edge sometime after 1879 (maps show that pre this date the brewery was set -back from the river). The arrow roughly indicates the level as to where the wort Cooler Pans were fitted, immediately above the Coolers were slatted vents set into the wall and on the roof and the latter are still in situ at the time of writing. These ventilators allowed the free circulation of air through the brewery and it was by this drawing of a draft across the shallow vessels (known as Cooler Pans or Flats) that held the hot wort (i.e. unfermented beer) that its required temperature reduction was brought about, when in use a considerable amount of steam would come up off the Cooler Pans and this would have been seen drifting out of the louvered vents.

Just visible in the above view is the brewhouse tower. This distinctive building also still stands and has become something of a local landmark, but again is it of any great age? Certainly the roof structure isn't as a photo taken about 1877 of the nearby railway shows the brewery in the background and at that date the brewhouse has a standard roof design, however, a photo of Caldewgate about 1898/99 (again with the brewery at a distance) confirms that by this date the brewery and brewhouse tower had been altered to the way it looks in the above 1971 photo. It is worth mentioning here about the Victorian cast iron 'liquor' i.e. water tank that was fitted in the top of the brewhouse tower. This vessel held the water which was to be used for brewing. Up to about 1920 the water was sourced and pumped up to the liquor tank from the well but in later years the brewery switched to using the cities piped supply, this vat was still in use right up until brewing ceased here in 1987.

Keeping on the subject of the brewery's Victorian fittings, the circle shown inside the brewhouse on the 1894/95 plan on the next page, which I have arrowed, was the position of the brewing Copper, it was about 10 feet deep and was built into a brick setting which not only served the purpose of supporting it but was fitted with a grate so that the Copper could be heated by coal firing from ground level, this action supplied the required heat to boil up the wort and the hops. This structure from ground level to the top of the Copper went some 16-18 feet up into the brewhouse and again this was another vessel that gave good service as it was still in use up until the brewery closed, though by the time Theakstons acquired the brewery it had been converted to steam boiling.

Below, a plan of the brewery as it was in 1894/95. Above, a photo taken in the brewery yard circa 1900 (more or less at the point marked **X** on the plan below).The view above shows part of the western elevation of the brewhouse and the whitewashed building was the malt and barley store, this scene altered about 1920 when a reinforced concrete extension was built onto the front of the brewhouse, this has had the affect of sealing in the old chimney stack, the remains of the whitewashed grain store were demolished about 1989.

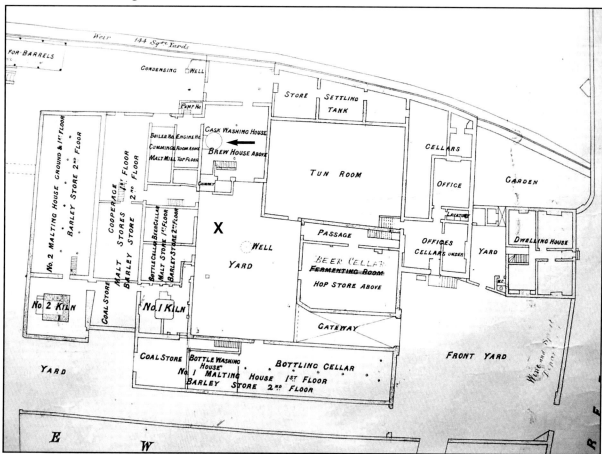

CARLISLE OLD BREWERY

It is a pity to say that some of the information about the fittings and workings of the Tun Room were sourced from an inquest into a fatal accident that occurred there on the night of 12 June 1899 (see Carlisle Journal report below).

SHOCKING ACCIDENT AT THE OLD BREWERY.

A WORKMAN DROWNED IN A TUN OF PORTER.

Last night a painful discovery was made at the Old Brewery, on the Caldew Bridge, the head cellarman, Robert Arnison, Granville Road, being found dead in one of the tuns used in the brewing of porter. It appears that about eight o'clock Joseph Thompson, an employé of the Old Brewery Company, was standing on Caldew Bridge when he observed that beer or porter was being rapidly discharged from one of the pipes into the Caldew, the quantity being so great that the river was discoloured and covered with froth for some distance. He at once suspected that something was wrong and ran into the brewery, where he called out Arnison's name. He received no reply, and proceeded upstairs to the tun room. The tuns are eight feet in depth, and Thompson saw that one of them, which had been half full of porter, had run almost empty. At the bottom, almost covered with porter and yeast, the deceased was lying motionless, face downwards. The liquid was still running away, but Thompson was quite powerless to do anything towards getting the body out on account of the deadly nature of the gas which is always present. Not only when there is a brewing in the tun but even after the liquid has been run off there is such an accumulation of carbonic acid gas in the tun that it would mean death to anyone entering it. Thompson, therefore, on making the shocking discovery at once took the only action which it was in his power to take. He ran for assistance, and called in Police-constable Taylor and others. A rope was procured and the deceased was drawn out. Steps were then taken to restore animation by promoting artificial respiration, but all the efforts which were made proved unavailing, and the body was subsequently removed by Police-constables Taylor, Steel, and Ellwood, to the Mortuary at the West Walls, where it will remain until the inquest is held. How the deceased got into the tun is a matter upon which there is at present nothing but speculation. The deceased's duty was to run the brewings off into the receptacles below, and it is surmised that one of the plugs had got wrong and that he was endeavouring to put it right when he overbalanced himself. A large bruise was found on his forehead, and his nose was broken. He had been in the employment of the Old Brewery Company for a considerable period, and was a steady and trusted worker. Much sympathy is felt with his wife and family under the painful circumstances.

In the subsequent inquest Roger Kendall, then the head brewer, gave information and his views on how Robert Arnison met his death.

'When deceased had emptied a vat he would knock-up the brass plug so as to wash out the sediment and yeast from the vat. He would go upstairs and turn water from a hose pipe into the vat to clean it out. A quantity of carbonic acid gas generates in the vats. Anyone entering a vat before it is washed out could not get out alive. Deceased nearly always wore clogs, my idea is that after deceased had ran off No.4 vat he by mistake knocked-up the brass plug in No.7 and finding his error rushed upstairs with a view to replace the plug. He would have to climb up to get into the Tun. There would be about 5 feet in depth of stout in No7 vat before the plug was knocked-up, the plug is from 4-5 inches in diameter there is a clear space beneath it, the stout would run onto the cellar floor direct and would quickly empty. There are some temperating pipes in the vat deceased might have hit his head against some of them. With the amount of gas in the vat deceased could not have got out and would not live long.'

Right: close up detail of the brewery's trademark. This is a 'fired-in' transfer on a stoneware bottle.

CARLISLE OLD BREWERY

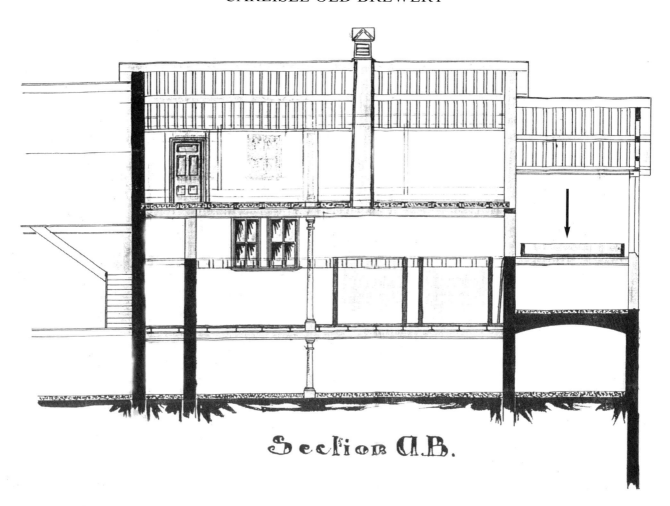

Section A.B.

Above, a section showing the design and layout of the intended new Tun room which was built in 1894. However, the architect's design wasn't exactly adhered to for the finished building's roof line and vents, as can be seen when this diagram is compared with the photo on page seven. The above also shows the layout of some of the brewing vessels, it being a section on line A - B through one of the three wort cooler pans (arrowed) and the front two fermentation vessels (also known as Tuns). The level of the wort cooler pan in the above diagram is also incorrect as it has been sited too low, there not been a sufficient drop for the cooled wort to be run out of this vessel down to the fermenting tuns, in reality the cooler pans would have been set at a slightly higher level (see arrow on photo page 7). Cooler vessels could be made from a number of materials e.g. wood or cast iron however copper being a good conductor was the most suitable for speeding up the required loss of heat in the wort. Close inspection of the above section indicates the cooler vessels and tuns were carried on girder joists, this would be necessary due to the considerable weight in these containers when full. Also it appears that no flooring boards were planned under the coolers, the reason for this must have been the fact that they would work quicker if a draft was allowed to play against the under side of the vessel as well as the top. Access to the cooler room was via ladders in the tun room, batten boards could be run across the joists for a man to stand on when there was a need to clean and flush out these vessels. Unlike other Victorian fittings these cooler pans were not in use during the brewery's final years and they must have been removed during the State Control period in favour of more modern cooling apparatus.

Finally a few details about the fermentation vessels/tuns shown in the above section and plan view on the next page. They were fitted new in 1894 and they were constructed of wood, probably oak or cedar as the latter is known for its rot resistance, but even so prolonged contact to moisture will eventually cause it to go stringy and spongy, so to aid cleaning and the prevention of infection getting into the brew it is known these tanks were lined with sheet copper on the inside, they were 8 feet deep and as would be expected, they were fitted with attemperating pipes (not shown in the section). They were still in use up to 1959 but by 1963 they had all been replaced with modern stainless steel fermenting vessels. It is known that the output of the Old Brewery in the 1912/14 period was just over 6,000 standard barrels per year and the average *Original gravity was 1041(the brand of beer carrying this o.g is not stated but it was very likely to have been the brewery's Mild).

*Original gravity, i.e. the specific gravity of the wort before fermentation, further references to this in the book will be abbreviated to o.g

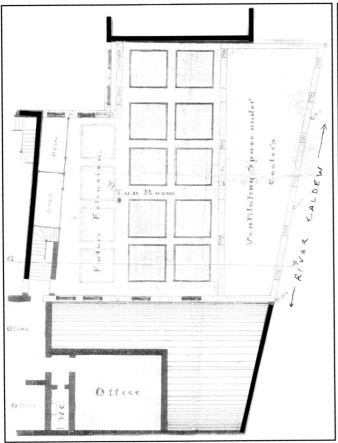

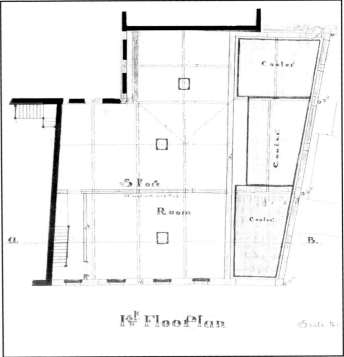

Above plan view of the cooler pans dating to 1894, to give some idea of the scale of these plans the combined length of the coolers ran to some 55 feet

Above, plan view of the layout of the fermenting vessels, totalling ten and having a dimension in feet of 8 x 8, the depth was also 8 feet, these F V's held between 45-50 barrels each and space has been left for 4 more to be fitted if necessary. The wording 'ventilating space', under coolers is a reference to the void under the pans that can be seen in the section on the previous page.

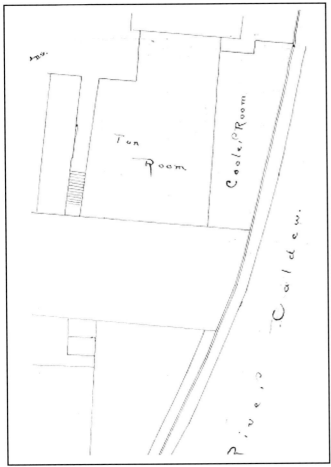

Left, a block plan showing the area of the brewery that the above plans and section relate to. This also corresponds to those buildings seen in the 1971 photo on page seven.

CARLISLE OLD BREWERY

Finally, who was Sir Richard Hodgson ? His name appears to always have been associated with the Carlisle Old Brewery right up to the State Management take over in 1916. All bottles and labels etc from the 1890's carried his name, and his family coat of arms, 3 birds (martlets) inside a shield, was used as the Carlisle Old Brewery Trade Mark even though this was some 85 years after he died.

Sir Richard Hodgson (1749-1806) was very much part of the early history of this brewery. He was the son of another Richard Hodgson (1708-79) a Carlisle mercer who was an original partner with James Atkinson establishing the brewery in 1756.

He was knighted in 1795, but it is not certain why. One possibility is that it was given for simply sending when Mayor, a congratulatory address from Carlisle on the escape of King George III from a mob that surrounded his carriage while on route to open parliament on 29 October 1794. Stones were hurled at the Royal coach and one went clean through the window, despite this ordeal it was said the King behaved with great coolness. Nevertheless this attack led to the Treasonable Attempts Bill.

Sir Richard was an Alderman of Carlisle, Mayor again in 1797 and High Sheriff of Cumberland in 1798.

A very rare example of a paper label circa 1894 which would have been stuck onto glass bottles. By the 1890's India Pale Ale was no longer just an export brand but had become popular as a bottled beer back home in Britain.
* Courtesy of Michael Jones British brewery label collection.

Stoneware stout bottles carrying a 'fired - in' Printed label were used by this firm from around 1890 up to the state takeover. EXTRA DOUBLE would have been a high gravity stout and possibly this particular brand was only supplied by the brewery in bottle.

CARLISLE NEW BREWERY
1774 - 1917

This view taken by Aerofilms on the 21 September 1925 shows that the brewery was still intact and seemingly unaltered from its block layout on the 1899 Ordnance Survey map, the brewhouse tower is arrowed and corresponds more or less in position to the letter marked A on the O.S. map (see next page). The trench like cut of the mill race and sluice gate referred to in the text can be seen in this view. Most of the site seen in the above photo is now occupied by Thomas Graham & Sons, steel merchants.

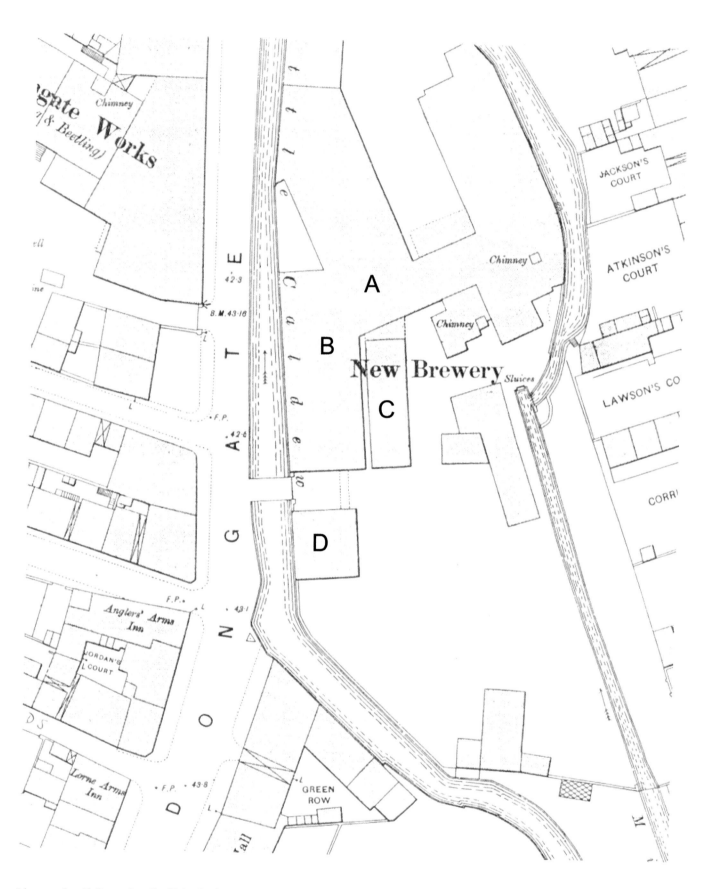

Above: detail from the Carlisle Ordnance Survey map of 1899, this can be compared with the photo on the previous page. Letter A was the position of the brewhouse tower, the buildings at B contained the malting floors, C was a bottling shed built new in 1893 and D was a new malting kiln built in 1894.

CARLISLE NEW BREWERY

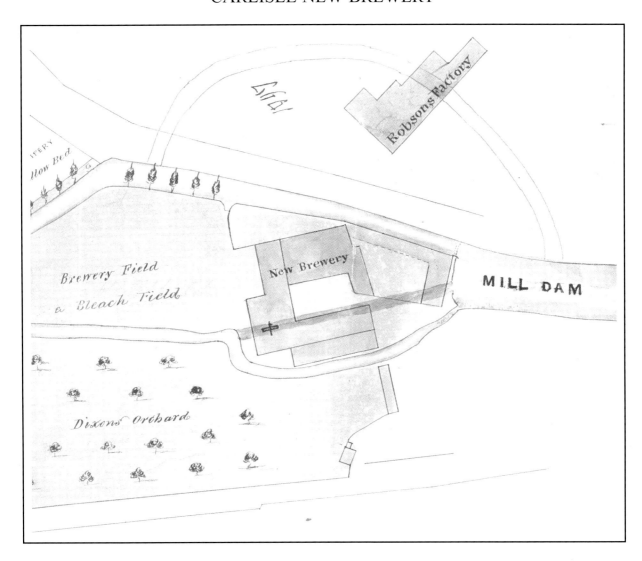

As no Victorian plans or records for this brewery are known to have survived, then unfortunately nothing can be said about its layout and fittings. However the site of the brewery and its close proximity to the mill race is worth considering because the works were purposely sited here to make use of water power, there being no suitable steam power then available to the brewing trade in 1774, the date this firm was established (the first steam engine to be fitted into a brewery was in London during 1784). The water wheel, which can be clearly seen marked on the map above would have been primarily used to power the mill in grinding the malted barley, the power for hoisting sacks of barley and hops, and in later years cranking mashing rakes, (machinery was introduced to replace man power in this part of the brewing process from around 1787). Also the wheel may have been linked to some sort of pumping mechanism to raise water up from the well.

The illustration above is taken from a larger map that was drawn sometime pre 1836. It records the industries that were sited along the stretch of the mill race between the New Brewery and back to what is now the vicinity of Junction Street. Between these points there were a number of other firms namely a dye works and corn mill that utilised water wheels. Robson's factory shown in the above illustration was concerned with the 'beatling' of cloth and was also a dye works, the bow shaped lines appear to have been an intended branch off the 'Little Caldew' mill race. Next to the factory are some figures which, although indistinct, could well be the date of the map, this looks to be 1797. If there is some doubt about this date what definitely can be said is that the map is pre 1836 as Dixon's factory and chimney which were completed in that year do not appear on it.

It is difficult to say when the water wheel would be dispensed with ,it could be that it was still in use even in the 1890's it being used in conjunction with steam power which had been fitted by then. There is some evidence for this as the sluice gate to allow water to run through the brewery is still marked on the 1899 Ordnance Survey map.

The output of the New Brewery during the 1912/14 period is recorded at around 6,300 standard barrels per year and the o.g of most of their beers at this time varied between 1042 -1043. The State Management ended brewing here in 1917 though malting and bottling continued at the site well into the 1920's. Today no trace of the New Brewery remains, its former site is now the location of Thomas Graham's steel merchants.

THE

New Brewery Company,

CARLISLE,

(LIMITED)

ESTABLISHED 1774.   INCORPORATED 1879.

𝕭𝖗𝖊𝖜𝖊𝖗𝖘 𝖆𝖓𝖉 𝕰𝖝𝖕𝖔𝖗𝖙𝖊𝖗𝖘 of

PALE ALES, BITTER BEER, & PORTER.

Brewery == Denton Holme, Carlisle.

T. H. PARKER, Manager.

Above: an advert taken from Arthur's 1880 street directory for Carlisle. The location given as Denton Holme is an error.

Above: demolition of the New Brewery had begun when this view was taken around 1973/74. This scene corresponds to those buildings marked B and D on the 1899 O.S. map, letter D being No 3 malting kiln.

GRAHAM'S QUEENS BREWERY
CALDEWGATE 1860-1916

Above: the Queens Head Inn. This photo was taken at the time of the coronation of King George V in May 1910.

It originally appeared in *A City Under The Influence* by John Hunt in 1971, but it has not been possible to trace the original photograph. Does it still exist?

Right: the 1899 O.S. map clearly showing the brewery behind the pub. The best way of understanding this map is to locate the Joiners Arms which is the only block of property still standing. The site of the brewery, Queens Head Inn and the Royal Oak is now occupied by Graham & Bowness' garage and showrooms.

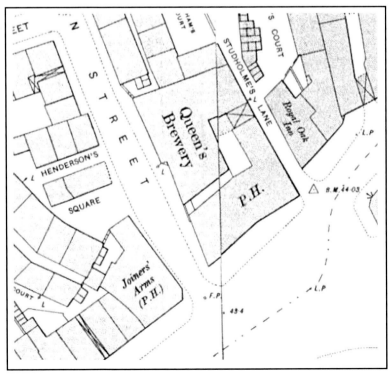

GRAHAMS QUEENS BREWEERY CALDEWGATE

At Graham's, as is the usual situation when attempting to study Carlisle's Victorian brewing trade, there is once again a lack of surviving records. What we do know is that the brewery was established in 1860 by Joseph Graham. The advert below from 1881 indicates he was not specifically a brewer by trade.

xxxvi   ARTHUR'S DIRECTORY OF CARLISLE.

JOSEPH · GRAHAM,
CHEMIST AND DRUGGIST,
GENERAL GROCER, AND TEA DEALER,
CALDEWGATE, CARLISLE.
THE QUEEN'S BREWERY,
XX and XXX DIAMOND ALES, &c.,
FAMILY WINE AND SPIRIT STORES,
Fisher Street, Newtown, and Church Street, Caldewgate,
CARLISLE.

According to an article written by John Minns in the *Carlisle Journal* of 1934 he briefly states that the brewery was 'first of all established to supply Mr Graham's own house* but developed rapidly.' This last statement seems a bit hard to justify as we know that structurally, when compared to the other Carlisle breweries, (after Hall's closed in 1898) it was the smallest. Grahams never owned more than 3 pubs these were 1. the City Vaults nick named the 'Klondike' and located in Fisher Street; 2. the Pedestrian Arms on Newtown Road and 3. the*Queens Head Inn fronting the brewery, also according to State Management records the brewery's output circa 1913 was about 1,900 standard barrels a year and this works out at barely 40 barrels a week. During the 1912-14 period the average o.g for the beers at Grahams was 1047. The State Management took over the brewery on the 7 September 1916 and brewing ceased there by the year's end.

The illustration to the right is from an advert that appeared in the *Carlisle Express and Examiner* on the 17.2.1912. 'IMPERIAL ALE' would have been a very strong bottle conditioned beer, being matured both in the cask then bottle for around a year before leaving the brewery. By the 1890's this was considered as the old - fashioned method of bottling, as bottled beers of a weaker gravity had become more popular and were turned out quicker than this.

2, Church Street,

CARLISLE. April 2nd 1894.

TO The Chairman & Directors,
        New Brewery Co., Ltd.,
            CARLISLE.

Gentlemen,

            Re - Practical Brewer & Malster wanted. Etc.

                    In reference to your advertisement for
Brewer etc., I have pleasure in offering you my services.

                    I may state for your information that I am married;
28 years of age, and that I have been continuously engaged,
for the last 13 years, in the Brewing trade.
                    I am thoroughly conversant with the different systems
of Malting, Brewing, Skimming, Cleansing, Squaring, etc. practis-
ed in all large Breweries.
                    For some time, I was an assistant Brewer at Dry-
brough's Brewery, Edinburgh (where the plant is a 50 quarter one),
under Mr R. Marshall, who is acknowledged to be one of the oldest
and most experienced Brewers in Scotland.
                    I have studied thoroughly the Chemistry of Brewing,
and am able to make a microscopical examination of yeasts etc.,
and all the different materials used in Brewing. I can also
determine the original specific gravity of any wort after fermentation.
                    In Drybrough's 3 Maltings of 25 quarters' capacity
each, I took an active share in the management, and also in the
sampling of barley for malting purposes.
                    I may also state that I flatter myself I can produce
First class Ales, Beers and Stouts of any gravity from 1028 to
1106, which cannot be beaten in this County.
                    The Brewing of Fine Pale Ales for barrel and bottling
purposes I have made a special study of, both for home and
foreign consumption.

Above: stoneware stout bottle, circa 1899

2.-

                    I was elected a member of the Institute of Brewing,
5 years ago, and still belong to that body.

                    I have pleasure in referring you to the following
gentlemen, who will testify to my capabilities of producing
articles suitable to the requirements of this district, of
which I need not inform you I am thoroughly acquainted:

            Mr R. Marshall, Chief Brewer, Drybrough's Brewery,
Edinburgh; Andrew Drybrough Esq., Brewery Owner, Edinburgh;
Mr Joseph Graham, 28, Castle St., Carlisle; Mr G. C. Toswell,
Messrs Spencer & Co., Brewers &c., Whitehaven; Mr Sinton and
Mr Gibson, Inland Revenue Officers, Carlisle.

                    Should you require any further information or
references, I shall be pleased to supply the same.

                    I remain,

                    Mr Chairman & Gentlemen,

                        Your obedient servant,

                            T. H. Graham

Thomas Graham's letter of application for the post of Practical Brewer & Maltster as wanted by the Carlisle New Brewery in 1894. The letter is evidence that he must have been proficient at his trade and includes a few details on the Queens Brewery's beers. Despite being well qualified he did not get the job and remained at his brewery. His father Joseph Graham died in 1902 and, as a result, he was in total charge of the factory until the end in 1916.

Above, an artist's impression of the brewery looking down Byron Street. This drawing is a fairly accurate representation of the works during the 1894-1916 period as it is based upon a distant Aerofilms view taken of the Caldewgate area in 1925 and also an architect's plan of the factory dated 1901. The building was a rather untypical looking brewery having no distinctive tower shaped brewhouse or large chimney stack. In fact it had more of a warehouse appearance, the out-building structure with the louvered vents was, according to the 1901 plan, the fermenting room, but the same drawing is vague in its detail about layout and fittings in the two taller buildings at its rear. X is the gable end of the Queens Head Inn. Despite the lack of detail about the internal layout and fittings it is thought likely that they would have been most professionally arranged and up to date as Thomas Graham, who was in charge of the brewing at this works by 1894, was probably the most skilled and capable brewer in Carlisle at that time, (see letter) on previous page.

Even though brewing ceased at Grahams during 1916 the brewery was not demolished until around 1928/29.

Right: paper label printed by Thurnam's
         about 1909.

IREDALE'S BREWERY
1876 - 1916

A splendid advertising card circa 1898 showing Iredales 1876 Currock Street brewery. Apart from the chimney it is an accurate representation of the factory as built. It was the most impressive of Carlisle's late Victorian breweries and its brewhouse and 110 foot chimney stack remained a Carlisle landmark until demolition occurred in 1975.

The 1899 O.S. map shows the brewery and the surrounding area. The best way for the reader to get his bearings is to use the present day 'Cumberland Wrestlers' as a guide. Today's pub is not the original as it was built in 1938, but it stands on the same position as the pub shown on the map. Also note the railway siding (arrowed) this was Mr Iredale's private siding, which the railway kept in for him in the deal of 1874. Interestingly it was actually a remnant of the original Newcastle and Carlisle Railway Canal Branch of 1837.

When the brewery was built it is possible that beer was exported using this rail-link, but there is no hard evidence to support this, what is certain is that it was used to bring coal to work the brewery and raw materials like hops and barley.

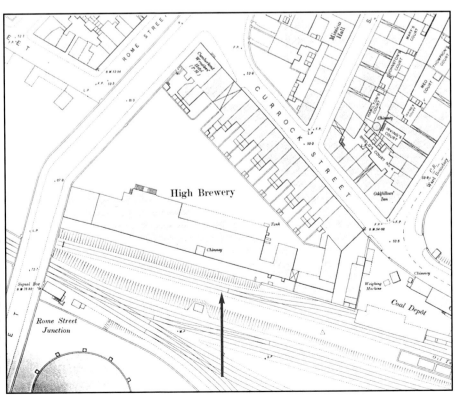

IREDALE'S BREWERY 1876 - 1916

The story of how the Currock/Rome Street brewery came to be built is directly linked to the need to extend the Citadel railway station, a decision taken by the London & North Western and Caledonian Railway companies around 1871. This extension in a South Westerly direction would require the demolition of some working class housing the Waterloo Foundry and also Iredale's earlier High Brewery situated in Water Street (see 1865 Ordnance Survey map below).

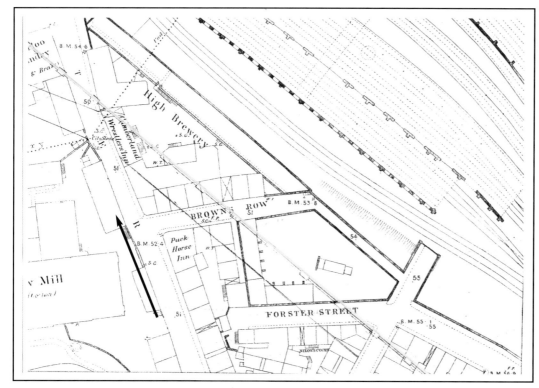

The 1865 O.S map. The yellow diagonal line marks the limit of the station extension completed in 1880. The map shows the brewery and surrounding area taken out by this development and the laying - in of a new road.

The Carlisle Journal 4.10.1878 reported that the destruction of condemned buildings in Water Street (arrowed) was making rapid progress.

The exact building date of the Water Street brewery is not known but it is thought to have been built during the 1820's and Joseph Iredale acquired the brewery around 1840. This, his first brewery, seems also to have been an impressive structure as it was described in 1862 'as one of the most complete breweries in the North of England'. Even if this was a rather exaggerated comment it could have been the most imposing of the earlier Carlisle breweries (unfortunately there are no known illustrations of this building). The brewhouse itself was 5 storeys in height, there were 11 fermentation vats of 20 - 25 barrels capacity each (4 of these were made from stone) and the brewery was capable of turning out 250 barrels of beer a week. But as mentioned this brewery could not remain, Iredale was aware of this by August 1871 when he had a valuation of his High Brewery and surrounding property taken, this being for a claim for compensation against the railway company for their intended compulsory purchase of his property; this came to £6,033. In fact Iredale had by this date already decided that he would continue in the brewing trade and that his cash claim was only part of the deal with the railway in that he wanted them to purchase the nearby site of the Currock Mill located at the junction of Currock Street and Rome Street where a 'very good well' was sited.

At this stage, he intended to just convert the old cotton mill into a brewery, also it is recorded, savings could be made by salvaging removable plant and fittings from his Water St brewery, such as the steam engine and boiler and possibly the Copper tank and resetting them in this building.

Proceedings between Iredale and the railway company seemed to have moved slowly as it was not until April 1874 that he got access to the Currock Mill site, but by now there had been a change of plan as it was decided to pull down the old mill and build a brand new brewery. Work to demolish and clear the site got under way immediately and the new brewhouse was under construction in April 1875, as the *Carlisle Journal* reported an accident when a bricklayer came off scaffolding breaking a leg. Despite this newspaper report the local press did not give coverage to the completion or the opening of Iredales new brewery and it seems to have started brewing without any publicity in the early months of 1876.

IREDALE'S BREWERY 1876 - 1916

So what details are known about Iredale's new 'HIGH BREWERY'. In a descriptive account of *Carlisle and its Industries* published in 1893, the brewery is described as 'a handsome four storied red brick building most substantially erected and equipped with steam hoists both within and without'. The Brewhouse as scaled off the original architects plan of 1874, stood 51 feet (that is ground level to the last course of brickwork) including the roof structure the overall height was around 65 feet.

As can be seen from the illustrations showing the brewery the central portion of the structure was given over to extensive malting floors which would have been labour intensive as the malt had to be aerated by turning with a shovel or fork. The barley germinates, the first sign of which is the appearance of growing roots and shoots. The roots grow, as does the shoot, but before growth has proceeded too far the grain, now known as 'green malt,' is put into a kiln (this is the building at the far right end of the brewery abutting Rome Street viaduct). Here the green malt was heated by hot air (the kiln was coal - fired) a process known as curing. This would last for a varying period and according to its duration and intensity would produce a pale or brown malt for brewing the different types of beers.

For further details relating specifically to the brewhouse itself we have to consider the architect's 1874 section/elevation plan of the brewery (see page 27). This is the only surviving plan of a Carlisle brewery and shows fittings and their layout, but can we trust that the internal arrangement of the brewing vessels, as seen in the plan, would in reality have been found exactly the same inside the finished brewery. The reason for bringing this point up is that they did not strictly adhere to the plan as far as the exterior was concerned. The chimney stack is completely different, circular on the plan, but when built it was square. Windows are shown in the southern elevation of the brewhouse on the plan, but were never put in, as demolition photos show a solid wall, and there are other discrepancies in the exterior between the plan and the real brewery.

However, accepting that the interior arrangement was adhered to, then here is a definite identification (bar object marked number 2) and description for the vessels marked on the section/elevation plan shown on page 27.

The shape marked number 1 on the elevation plan was the Grist case/hopper. This fed the mashing apparatus with ground/milled malt. The object arrowed 2 on the section plan appears to be a small water tower (not unlike those found on the railway used for filling up steam loco tenders), presumably circular and supported on a column. It is possible that this vessel served a dual purpose, receiving cold water directly from the well and being fitted with steam pipes, it heated up the water ready for use in the Mash Tuns sited below. However it could not be described as a conventional piece of brewery plant as I have not seen anything like this in other Victorian brewery plans.

From the Mash Tuns (No 3 on the plan) the liquid now known as Wort is run down to the Copper (No 4) where hops are added and a lengthy boiling takes place. Looking at the location of the Copper in this brewery plan indicates that it was sited quite high up the brewhouse in fact the bottom of the vessel is some 23 feet off the ground. It also appears to be fitted in between two floors. There is no brickwork support indicated so it must have been carried on girder joists (one is shown on the plan) as the copper metal vessel itself could not be fixed directly it would have to be in some sort of wrought iron frame or case and it would be this that was bolted on to the girders.

It could be that the setting of the Copper and Hop - Back at this level was to allow the brewery's steam boiler to be located directly below on the ground floor (i.e. the void arrowed 10 on the section), so by this arrangement the Copper would be heated by a steam pipe running vertically off the boiler. During the 1870s when Iredales brewery was being built, steam boiling of Coppers was promoted by brewery designers and engineers as a modern and more efficient improvement over direct coal fired Coppers, though they never widely caught on in Britain before 1900.

Another point when considering the height of the Copper and Hop Back(No 5) is that they are just above the level of the Cooler Pan (No 6) located in the opposite tun room building so the hot wort would have taken little or no pumping across to this vessel, unlike some brewery lay-outs that had a Copper in a brick setting coal fired from low down in the brewery or at the ground level and as a result had to pump the hot wort a vertical distance back up to its Coolers.

Despite some doubt that the lay out of the brewery fittings (and that one of these is non standard) seen in the plan turned out to be the real arrangement in the brewery when built, it does appear that the intended floor levels were followed. The evidence for this can be seen in the 1975 demolition photo on page 29 which shows a doorway some 16 feet up the brewhouse, an opening at about the same level is confirmed on the 1874 plan (not shown on the section/elevation on p27) and led from the floor where the hop-back was intended to be placed to the top floor of the Tun room building opposite, via a linking gangway.

The Hop Back at Iredale's seems to have been a long, trough like, tank 3-4 feet deep. They had been made of wood but by the 1870's most British breweries had a cast iron vessel. The Hop-Back was basically a sieve and was fitted with removable perforated cast iron plates that acted as a strainer whereby the leaf hop debris and other material would be held back whilst the hot wort would pass through to the cooler pan. The Hop Back level is just above the cooler in the opposite building on the plan and it looks as if it was packed on wooden blocks to enable a slight fall to be gained in draining the hot wort across to the cooler pan in the Tun room.

Cooler pans have been referred to previously and at Iredales only one large pan was fitted. It is not recorded what the cooler was made from, but copper, though expensive, was the best material. Slate, cast iron and even cement were also used in other breweries.

At Iredales to further assist cooling the wort and to speed the whole process up, especially during the summer months, was the use of a vessel known as a Horizontal Refrigerator (arrow 8 on the section plan). The word 'refrigerator' could be misleading for the reader, as this was not an ice making machine, nor was it electrically powered. It was though, an affective heat exchanger. See diagram below.

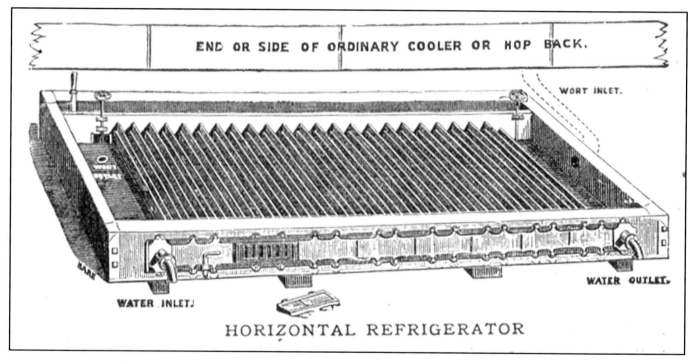

HORIZONTAL REFRIGERATOR

The cold well water enters the apparatus and traverses through the thin tinned copper tubes in a zigzag fashion, gradually absorbing the heat of the wort until it exits as warm water . The Wort itself would run into the refrigerator falling about a foot from the Cooler at about 80°F running under and over the cold water tubes until it exits at around 58-60°F down to the Tuns. It was this piping of the cold water counter current (i.e. in the opposite direction to that of the warm wort) that was the key to the success in this apparatus.

The Refrigerator shown above was patented by Robert Morton in 1862. It was widely used and a large number were fitted in British breweries during the 1870's. Though Morton's refrigerator was generally regarded as the best available there were variations on the same design marketed by other firms. The refrigerator used at Iredales was, like the cooler pans that they were often used in conjunction with, quite shallow being only 8 - 12 inches deep, but 25 feet in length by 8 feet wide.

Once the wort had been cooled down to the required temperature of around 58 - 64°F it was run into the fermentation vessels also known as 'Tuns'. These were located on the floor directly beneath the cooler and refrigerator (arrow 7 on the section plan). No detail about what these tuns were made from is recorded, or their capacity. The section through the tun room floor is very poorly detailed.

Jumping now to the known details about the end product itself i.e. the brands and gravities of Iredales beer.It seems four types were produced regularly from 1876 to the State takeover in 1916. These were described in 1879 as; 1. Strong beer, 2. Bitter beer (by 1893 this was often referred to as Australian or XXX), 3. Mild ale and 4. Stout. Gravities of three of these drinks are recorded in 1879 as follows. 1. Strong beer o.g. 1083, 2. Bitter beer o.g. 1069, 3. 'Common' i.e. Mild ale o.g. 1063.

It should be pointed out here that the original gravities of British beer were generally stronger during the 1870's compared to the 1890's, the average o.g. for beer in Cumberland at 1899 was 1050 and, by the outbreak of World War 1, the average o.g. of British beer was down to 1046. It is recorded that the average gravity at Iredales brewery around 1914 was 1045, though the beer type with this o.g. is not recorded but I would think it would be the brewery's Mild, as this would have been the weakest of the 4 beer types.

Recorded comments on Iredale's beer in 1893, are as follows, it was said to enjoy ' a very high reputation for its Strong and Bitter Beers, Mild Ales and Stout which are of the highest order of purity and excellence. The leading speciality of the house consists in its celebrated Australian Bitter Beer and Mild Ale brands which stand particularly high in popular estimation wherever they are introduced. The firm have also specialities in Invalid Stout.'

It is recorded that the trade in 1876 -1879 was only 60-100 barrels a week even though the works was capable of brewing 300-500 barrels a week. Iredales tied -pub trade in Carlisle at this time was just 7 pubs (though he had 2 or 3 properties on the rural outskirts) and it never exceeded 10 Carlisle pubs during the 1894 -1916 period. Years later, when the State Management took over the brewery, output was still well under capacity at just 86 barrels a week.

The brewery seen from Rome Street viaduct in 1974/75. The elevated grass embankment had been the site of Iredale's railway siding.

IREDALE'S BREWERY 1876 - 1916

In early 1876 when the brewery started production Joseph Iredale was 70 and his whole life had been dedicated to brewing. He was born at Low Hollins farm in the Lorton valley near Cockermouth in 1806 (incidentally the same area that produced the Jennings of Cockermouth brewery fame) and it was said that he had 'realised a considerable fortune out of the brewery trade,' but by 1879 his new brewery was up for sale. The reason for this (sourced from documents at that time) seems to have been 'his desire to retire from hard work', but more notably a rift or disagreement with his two sons whom he had hoped would succeed him in running the brewery and actively expand the trade. But Iredale via his solicitor had this to say about them: 'he has been disappointed, as neither of them are turning out so well as they might do and he finds they are going to be of no assistance to him and, as he is now above 70 years of age, these concerns have induced him to consider the advisability of parting with the business and property in his lifetime, instead of leaving it to be wasted after his death.' Also, from the same letter: ' there is no doubt but that the trade might be enormously increased by a younger and more active man. Had Mr Iredale been 20 years younger or had his sons been what he would like to see them, then the property would never have come on the market.'

 This personal family detail comes from correspondence between Iredale and his solicitor with the potential purchaser, Mr G. Wadley of Norwood in Surrey. Mr Wadley had been the Head Brewer at the City Of London brewery and it was said he had ample means to carry out the purchase (Iredale was wanting between £20-25,000 for the brewery). This transaction though never took place despite fairly detailed correspondence between the two parties and Mr Wadley acknowledging 'that the brewery and maltings are modern and good.'. The problem seems to have been over the amount of tied properties Wadley would receive for the purchase price,as Iredale was only prepared to sell 2 of his 7 Carlisle public houses. This proposed sale of the brewery seems to have been a private treaty as the brewery sale advert is not recorded in the local press. Joseph Iredale died just two years later in 1881 at his house in Portland Square. One of his sons, of whom he was so critical during 1879, did however continue running the business until F.P. Dixon (grandson of the Peter Dixon of Dixon's chimney fame) became managing director of the brewery in 1889 (he had married a daughter of Joseph Iredale).

  Surprisingly, despite the brewery being fairly modern and having a good potential capacity the State closed it in 1916 .The only reason that I can think of for this action is that Iredales brewery site location was somewhat cramped and restricted, if there was ever a need for any future building extensions. However, the brewery was retained as stores and all the buildings remained intact, but with the demise of the State Management scheme in 1971 there was no further use for the brewery. It was then let for a rifle range (in the malting floors) and a decorators workshop but, with most of the building unoccupied, it soon became a target for vandals. In November 1974 there was a serious fire and demolition came in the summer of 1975.

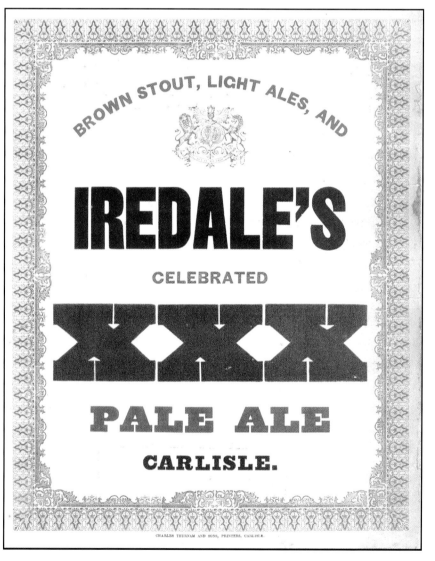

BROWN STOUT, LIGHT ALES, AND

IREDALE'S

CELEBRATED

XXX

PALE ALE

CARLISLE.

CHARLES THURNAM AND SONS, PRINTERS, CARLISLE.

IREDALE'S BREWERY 1876 - 1916

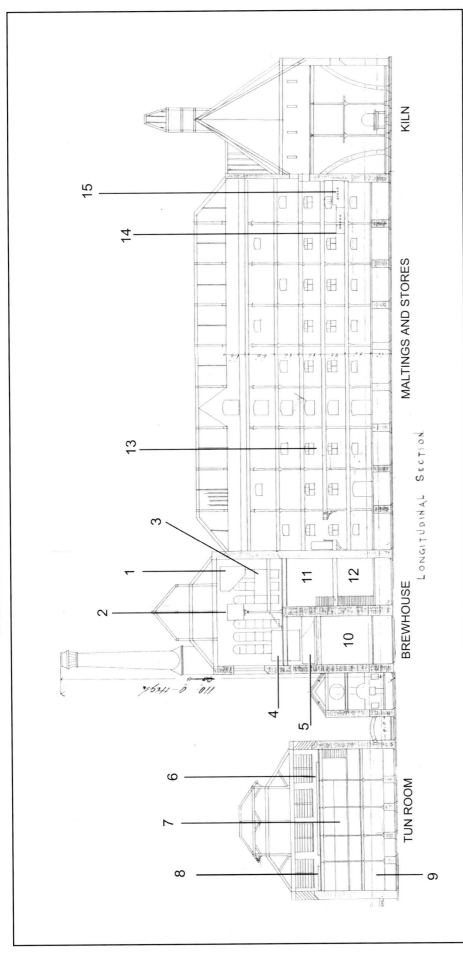

LONGITUDINAL SECTION

TUN ROOM · BREWHOUSE · MALTINGS AND STORES · KILN

Above, the 1874 section plan for Iredales intended new brewery. The architect was Carlisle's Daniel Birkett who later designed the Central Hotel in 1879. I have marked a numbered key on the plan to guide the reader with the lay-out and fittings (this plan is also referred to in the text). The structure between the brewhouse 'tower' and tun room building was not actually built and the tun room itself was pulled down before the rest of the brewery between 1963-73.

1. Grist Case, this was a storage hopper sited above the Mash Tun, which supplied crushed malt ready for mashing. **2.** Liquor (i.e. water tank?), an unusual design and certainly not a typical Victorian brewery fitting. **3**. section through one of the two 8 quarter Mash Tuns. **4.** Copper, this was according to the scale on the original plan 9 feet deep and 9 feet in diameter. **5.** Hop Back. **6.** Cooler Pan. **7.** Tuns/Fermentation Vessels located in this area. **8.** Horizontal Refrigerator. **9.** Racking cellar, 6 foot headroom. **10.** Likely a coal fired steam boiler located in this void. **11.** Likely position of Malt Mill and elevator running vertically up to feed the grist hopper. **12.** Likely position of steam engine machinery. **13.** one of the malting floors. **14.** Couch, a rectangular wooden boarded frame which contained the barley grain to a depth of about 3 foot after it had been removed from the Steep tank, the idea of 'Couching' was to encourage germination in the grain by allowing some heat to build up in it before it was spread out on the floors. **15.** Steep, a water filled tank where the grain was soaked, the main purpose of the 'Steep' was also to promote germination.

IREDALE'S BREWERY 1876 - 1916

A longitudinal view of the 1876 brewery taken from the yard around 1974. The building from this angle can be compared with the architects section plan and also the coloured advertising card on page 21. We have had to 'stitch' this photo together as the original cameraman did not have a wide angle lens which would have given us the entire length of the building in one view, this accounts for the slight distortion in the above image, (though if you had drunk 4 or 5 pints of Iredales XXX Bitter you probably wouldn't notice the difference). Joking aside, note the rather Gothic styled narrow tower connected to the maltings, this enclosed a steam - powered hoist or elevator for moving the barley, malted barley and hops around the different levels. The projecting building with the flight of steps was the brewery office, originally with a clock above the door. The X X X was Joseph Iredales Trade Mark and 3 of these heavy fireclay slabs still survive in the stores at Carlisle Museum; metal X signs were also fixed to the chimney and brewhouse. The brewery was described by Iredale in 1879 as a 16 'Quarter' plant.

Above, Iredale's brewhouse in the summer of 1975 and demolition is just days away. This photo shows the southern wall of the brewhouse 'tower.' It stood some 46 -51 feet from the ground to the the last course of bricks. When the roof structure was included, its overall height was around 65 feet. Note the doorway some 16 feet up the building. This is the opening referred to in the text which led to where the Hop Back was located.

 According to the 1874 architect's plan, windows were to be fitted into this wall of the brewhouse, but as can be seen this was not carried out. The chimney height is given as 110 feet on the plan, but on this it is shown as a circular stack, which again was not adhered to when the brewery came to be built. While on the subject of the chimney, note that it was built into the brewhouse and the internal intrusion of the stacks brickwork must have cut down the available space.

HALL'S CROWN BREWERY
1869-1898

Of the five Carlisle breweries trading in 1894 then Hall's has left the least trace of its existence in the way of records and clues to its appearance. It was called the Crown Brewery after the Crown Hotel and it was here that David Hall (senior) had established himself as manager and licensee about 1850. But in later years running the licensed premises was not his only living as, by 1865, he was recorded as a builder, joiner and innkeeper. The following year saw David Hall bankrupt at the Newcastle and District Court having debts of £1,500, lost mostly on betting. This was not the end of the family connection with the Crown Street site as David (junior), William and Lowingham made good his debts and David (senior) appointed his eldest son Lowingham to superintend his business.

Then in the *Carlisle Journal* 9 July 1869 appeared the following advert:

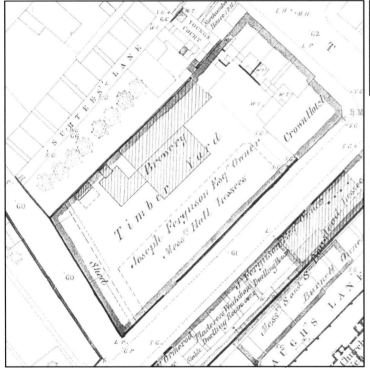

CROWN BREWERY, CARLISLE.
D. HALL & SONS having had the above Brewery fitted up with the most approved appliances, beg to inform their Friends and the Public that they are producing ALES, BEER, and PORTER of unsurpassed quality, and are prepared to execute orders to any extent.

Left , detail of the 1865 Ordnance Survey map for this area of Carlisle. The plan of the brewery has been added in pen to the map at a later date confirming that it must have been built after 1865. The land on which the brewery was built and the Crown Hotel belonged to Joseph Ferguson a Carlisle architect and the Halls were lessees. But it does seem they erected the brewery and fitted it out at their own expense.

 Considering now the products of the brewery; John Minns, writing years later in 1934, recalled in an article in the Carlisle Journal about the drinks trade pre - State Management that; ' a brewery known as Hall's was erected behind the hotel and was famous for its products.' It is likely that this statement should be taken in the context of the beer being popular and sought after in Carlisle and not nationally. It is known that pre -1890 Hall's supplied the Malt Shovel the London & North Western Railway Inn, the Oddfellows and the Goliath.

 During the 1870- 1890 period, there were more privately owned 'free houses' in Carlisle but by the late 1890's this situation had changed as the Carlisle Old ,New and Maryport breweries had bought up many pubs (including 3 of the previously mentioned) and as a result had a considerable tied trade .This could well have contributed to the demise of the Crown brewery as its outlets were diminished. Possibly they couldn't or weren't prepared to compete financially in acquiring a tied estate, though the size of the brewery would have eventually restricted that anyway, whatever there seems to have been no interest by Lowingham Hall in keeping the brewery open when the lease expired during the summer of 1898. It seems the lease was not renewable, but presumably Ferguson would have given the Halls the option of buying the land. This arrangement would surely have been written into the legal documents drawn up in 1868/69, when the Halls built their brewery on his ground.

 However, in the summer of 1898 the lease on the Crown Hotel was also about to expire. Lowingham Hall would have been aware that it was going to be offered for sale and it was this property, not the brewery, that a decision was taken to try and secure. That the hotel was regarded as more important to retain than the brewery suggests that by this time there was no financial benefit in keeping the Crown Brewery trade running, and that the ownership of the hotel was more of a priority. As it turned out, Hall just missed acquiring the Crown hotel when it came up for auction in the September of that year (even though he bid up to £11,300) and this episode had the result of ending the long association of this family's name with the site.

HALL'S CROWN BREWERY 1869-1898

Right, this advert appeared in the *Carlisle Journal* newspaper in May 1898. It is not clear whether the brewery was being offered as a going concern. If so there were no takers as there are no records of it trading after this sale and it is not marked as a brewery in the following year when the 1899 Ordnance Survey for Carlisle was carried out, though the building itself was still standing. Some of the fittings would likely have been sought after by local brewers for either re-use or spares, or the somewhat obvious alternative was that much of the equipment was simply stripped out and sold for scrap.

The advert is interesting as to the amount of detail that is given on the brewery's equipment. The comment by Hall's back in 1869 that the brewery was fitted up with the most approved appliances is borne out by the mention of Steel's patent masher and Morton's patent refrigerator. These particular pieces of brewing equipment were at the time generally regarded as the best in the industry and would have been quite expensive to have installed. Interestingly there was actually a Carlisle firm manufacturing brewers plant during the late Victorian period. This was Pratchitt Bros engineers at their Denton Holme works. In 1881 they manufactured refrigerators along with coolers, hop-backs, mash tubs, cast iron water tanks and other brewery equipment.

Returning to the subject of the 1898 advert again, there does seem to be an error which should be noted. According to it the breweries fermenting tuns, had a capacity of only 90 gallons, or put another way each fermentation vessel held the ridiculously small amount of just two and half barrels each. This is very likely incorrect as other details that are given in the above newspaper notice conflict with the brewery having such a small capacity. It is far more likely that a nought was somehow omitted off this figure when the detail for the advert was originally placed with the printer. So very likely the real capacity of these Tuns/F.V's was 900 gallons each, i.e. each one held 25 barrels. It is likely that the works could set up brewings to the amount of 100 barrels a week of which about half of this quantity would be 'racked off,' that is filled into barrels per week (Monday -Monday).

Over the years this brewery produced the usual range of beers common to most other establishments in Victorian Britain, but in 1875 it is worth mentioning a type then being offered called 'Ruby Strong Ale' at 80 shilling a barrel. The reference to a 'ruby' would almost certainly have been in connection to the colour of this particular beer. Also, in an advert in the Carlisle Journal for 23 May 1890, Halls stated that they were brewing 'Stout on the Dublin principle and it is now in splendid condition'.

Finally if any descendants of the Halls or in fact any reader has old records, plans/maps, labels, advertisng or prints relating to this brewery then please let me know as I would very much like to get a copy of such. I can be contacted via the address given on page 3 of this book.

CROWN BREWERY, CROWN STREET, BOTCHERGATE, CARLISLE.

IMPORTANT SALE OF BREWERY PLANT, BEER BARRELS, HORSES, CARTS, &c.

CASTIGLIONE and GIBBINGS are favoured with instructions from Mr. Hall (in consequence of expiration of lease) to Sell by Auction on the Premises as above, on THURSDAY, JUNE 2nd, the whole of his BREWERY PLANT, FITTINGS, HORSES, CARTS, &c., briefly as follows :—

Five quarter Brewing Plant, 6-Horse-power Engine, boiler 9ft. 6in. by 3ft. 6in., with Steam Pipes and connections ; Settling Square 13ft. by 8ft. by 2ft., with Cooling Pipes, equal to new ; 2 Fermenting Tuns, capacity about 90 Gallons each ; 5 Quarter Mash Tuns, Cast-iron Underback Force Pump, with Shafting, Pulleys, Pipes, and Fittings ; Steel's Patent Masher, Copper Boiler 6ft. diameter by 6ft. deep, 2 Iron Girders 11ft. by 1ft. 9in., 2 do. 7ft. by 1ft. 9in., large Wrought-iron Boiler, Cast-iron Cistern 12ft. by 8ft. by 3ft. 3in., with Oak and Red Wood Supports ; Iron Cooler 15ft. 6in. by 18ft. 6in. by 9in. deep, Morton's Patent Refrigerator 14ft. 6in. by 6ft., with Copper Fittings ; Weighing Machine by Garland, quantity of Boarding forming Malt and Hop Rooms, Copper Attemporator, Hop Press, Malt or Grain Mill.

BEER BARRELS AND CASKS.—15 Hogsheads, 200 Barrels, 150 Half Barrels, 80 Quarter Casks, Shakes and Staves, Bottling Machine, Bottle Washer, Gantries, Ladders, Wood Sheds 47ft. by 15ft., do. 58ft. by 10ft., do. 12ft. by 6ft. by 7ft., do. 22ft. by 9ft., do. 15ft. by 11ft., a large quantity of Lead Piping to be sold by weight.

3 Cwt. of Kent and Worcester HOPS, Half-cwt. of SACCHARINE.

HORSES, CARTS, &c.—Bay Cart Horse, 10 years old, 16½ hands high, a good stamp ; Grey Harness Horse, 12 years old, 15 hands high, a useful sort ; Brewer's Cart, Brewer's Dray ; Gig by Proud, Carlisle ; Spirit Merchant's Spring Cart, Set of Gig Harness, Set of Van Harness, Set of Cart Gear, Stable Utensils, and other Effects.

The above is only a brief outline of the Lots for Sale.

Sale at 1 p.m. prompt with Plant, Barrels, &c. be sold after the Plant, Barrels, &c.

The attention of Brewers is called to the Plant and Barrels as they are all in good order.

CARLISLE PUBLIC HOUSES
1894-1916

In 1894 there was a total of 114 properties in the city that retailed beer, wines and spirits which could be drunk inside the premises. These type of properties were classed as 'ON' licenses, they ranged from large sized hotels down to back- street pubs. There were also a further 9 pubs that had an 'ON' licence, better known as 'Beer Houses' but, as their name suggests, that was the only type of drink they sold, not having a 'Full' license to sell wines and spirits.

Finally, there was an additional 6 Beer Shop 'Off licenses' where customers obtained bottle and jug carryouts.

The large city hotels, namely the Great Central, Bush, County, Red Lion, Crown & Mitre and the Turf (located at the Swifts racecourse), are hardly the type of properties that spring to mind when the term public house is mentioned, so they are omitted from this survey. Equally the off licenses can not be classed as public houses as consumption of drink was not allowed on the premises. There were six of this type of licensed house in Carlisle at this time and four of them also doubled as grocers' shops and little is known about their history. Despite the lack of illustrations for these properties the following brief details are given about them.

Their location is worth considering as five of them were virtually clustered together; being just off Botchergate and London Road. This district bounded by Union Street (now Rydal Street), Fusehill and Lindisfarne Streets, enclosed a large block of Victorian working-class housing, a typical area wherein you would expect to find corner street pubs. Yet with the exception of one short lived pub, namely the 'Smiths Arms' in Union Street which was closed in 1874, and the late arrival (built 1900) of the rather out of place looking Linton Holme Hotel, these back-street pubs were never established. In comparison, consider the smaller working-class district of terraced housing around Crown Street and Currock Street, then known as the 'Wapping'. There in 1894 were situated six pubs virtually in a stone's throw of one another. So what caused the lack of pubs in the Fusehill and Greystone Road areas? It seems the likely answer lies with the date when much of this area was built, because, other than Union Street, most of the rest of this area went up after 1870. By this time the local magistrates were back in control of public house licensing and a course of action restricting the granting of new licenses was adopted. It can be no coincidence that only four pubs were constructed on green-field sites in Carlisle between 1870 and 1916. These were the Moulders Arms and Cumberland Wrestlers in Currock Street, both going up circa 1875, followed by the Currock Hotel built in 1899 and the Linton Holme Hotel built in 1900. Yet this can be set against a time of considerable urban development, with much building work going on, not only in the Fusehill area but also in the Denton Holme and Currock districts.

The years 1890-95 were a difficult period for the licensing trade nationally. In a letter to the *Carlisle Journal* 19 April 1892, J.B Towerson, the owner of the Wigton brewery, complained about the current licensing situation and there is evidence from his letter that he personally thought that a state of prohibition on the drinks trade was not far off. It was thought likely that many areas of the country could indeed have gone 'dry' if the Liberals had been returned to power in the General Election year of 1895. There were others during the 1890's who advocated Nationalisation of the liquor trade as the next best choice in dealing with the social problems caused by drink. One idea put forward during 1894 by the aptly named Dr Beveridge of Aberdeen was the municipalisation of the liquor traffic. The *Carlisle Journal* during 1898, commented about the policy adopted by the magistrates of granting very few new licenses in the city and 'losing no reasonable opportunity of reducing the number of old ones'. There is little doubt that in some areas of Victorian Carlisle there were too many public houses, particularly Rickergate and the old city centre and it was in these localities that nearly all the Victorian and Edwardian pub closures took place. During the period covered by this book, 24 Carlisle pubs were closed and this was even before the State Management arrived to wield its axe, though it should be pointed out that this regime shut 17 Carlisle pubs in just one year (i.e.1916).

Returning to the subject of the licensed grocers shops located in the back-streets off Botchergate and London Road. It seems these type of properties were acceptable to the licensing authorities and there must have been some demand for a carry-out trade in the area to have supported five of them. This is backed-up by an article in the *Carlisle Journal* on the 10 September 1897, when they reported about an off - license located at the corner of Fusehill and South Streets which had been expected to fetch £700 but was actually sold to the Carlisle New Brewery for £2,675 after they had got into a bidding match with a rival brewery. The report went on to say ' the beerhouse happens to be placed in a position in which it is a great convenience to householders of the district and has the practical monopoly of that particular trade'.

Incidentally this shop is still trading today and alcoholic drinks still form part of their stock. The other four in this area during the 1890's though are long gone, they were located at 87 Union Street (this was purchased for £1,000 by the Workington Brewery Co in 1897); 13 Edward Street (tenanted by a Mary Telford); 34 Orchard Street (owned or tenanted by James& Hannah Nixon) and 5 Orchard Street, Robert and Jane Thompson beer retailers. The other beershop off licence in the city at this time was located at the junction of Blackwell Road and Boundary Road (also known locally as 'Five roads end' see circa 1905 photo below) and was then tenanted by William Finlay who was also a grocer.

In 1893 the Carlisle New Brewery tried to acquire this property, Finlay told them 'he was prepared to take all the draught ale, porter and beer he required, say one barrel per week on an average for the 'jug trade', but as far as bottled beer was concerned he bottled Allsops and would not change'. By1900 Finlay had stocked up with glass bottles embossed with his own name and, for some reason, they carried a star trade mark.

Of the 117 properties in 1894 (this figure does not include the 6 Hotels previously referred to), licensed to sell drink to be consumed on the premises, 60 of them appear in the following pages and some known history is given on each one of them and a full list of all 123 'ON' licensed properties in Carlisle at this date can be found at the back of the book. A further two properties namely the Currock and Albert Hotels are also covered, even though they were not on the licence register of 1894, nevertheless, as their history is little known about, they have been included. These 62 pubs are arranged in the order of where they were located rather than treating them alphabetically.

Before ending this introduction, the term 'Spirit Vault' needs to be explained. This word when used by the Ordnance Survey to mark some licensed properties on its maps of 1865 and 1899, means the pub was then in occupation by a wine and spirit merchant and at these dates was then not trading under or displaying a name or sign. However, the very same term was displayed by publicans on some of the city's named pubs (see Cumberland Wrestlers on p.54). These properties rarely had a connection to wine and spirit merchants and were 'tied' to the local brewers. The meaning of the term here was to make clear that this was a pub that stocked spirits, in other words the pub had a 'full licence,' By displaying the wording 'Spirit Vault' the pub could be easily recognised as not being a beerhouse. This type of advertising would have been aimed at attracting the passing trade of customers who were not local to the area, or from outside of Carlisle.

CALDEWGATE AREA

Above, a view of Caldewgate about 1910. The property in the foreground was the 'Queens Head Inn' the brewery was located at the rear of the pub (see p 17). Note the board sited on the gable indicating the direction down Byron Street to Creighton's saw mill, the camera angle just misses the Joiners Arms.

The following is a list of all the public houses located in this area in 1894, those printed in bold are covered in detail in the following pages. Milbourne Street pubs are classed under this area rather than Denton Holme.

1.	**JOVIAL SAILOR**	NEW SAILOR BUILT 1904 STILL OPEN
2.	**PLOUGH INN**	CLOSED CIRCA 1918 PULLED DOWN BY1954
3.	**JOINERS ARMS**	STILL OPEN
4.	QUEENS HEAD	CLOSED CIRCA 1918
5.	**ROYAL OAK**	OFF LICENSE BY 1920 PULLED DOWN 1987
6.	OLD ANCHOR	PULLED DOWN 1901
7.	**WILLIAM JAMES**	CLOSED 1912
8.	GLOBE	STILL OPEN
9.	**WAGGON AND HORSES**	CLOSED 1917 PULLED DOWN 1924
10.	**MALTSTERS**	CLOSED AND PULLED DOWN 2004
11.	**BRICKLAYERS ARMS**	CLOSED 1916 PULLED DOWN 2001
12.	PHEASANT	CLOSED 1999
13.	ANGLERS ARMS	CLOSED 1916
14.	**LORNE ARMS**	CLOSED CIRCA 1919
15.	**DUKE OF YORK**	CLOSED 2000
16.	**MILBOURNE ARMS**	STILL OPEN
17.	**WOOLPACK**	STILL OPEN
18.	SPINNERS ARMS	CLOSED CIRCA 1919

JOVIAL SAILOR

The 1894 register lists the Jovial Sailor but at that date it was a totally different property (see below) compared to the one that stands in the same vicinity today.

Above, the original Jovial Sailor at 34 Caldcotes. Its location was in a terrace of properties described in 1902 as cottages. It is difficult to be certain when these were built, however the first reference to it as the Sailor occurs in 1837. The significance of its naming was almost certainly linked to the presence of the nearby ship canal of 1821-1853. The photo was taken on Christmas day 1903 and shows the tenant John Nichols. The pub at this time was owned by the Carlisle New Brewery.

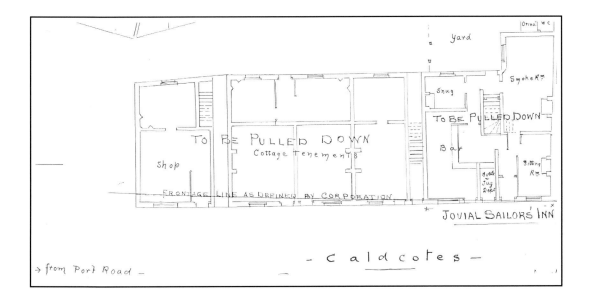

The above plan dates to 1902 and shows the position of the original Jovial Sailor. By February 1902 the New Brewery Co that owned this block of property took the decision to have it pulled down in order to construct a modern larger public house and shops on this site. The demolition started in the spring of 1903 with the original Sailor being the last to go in the February or March 1904, when today's pub first opened for trade.

Above, the 1902 architect's elevation showing the intended new Jovial Sailor and what was planned to be shops. This can be compared with the recent photo below and as can be seen the architect's plan for the new Jovial Sailor was accurately followed (the sills on the arched windows were raised by the state management between the wars). However, the section of property intended to be shops was not adhered to and instead became the small terrace of houses as seen below.

The Jovial Sailor in November 2002, as referred to previously it first opened for trade around February 1904 The position of the original Sailor was where the last two houses in this block now stand.

PLOUGH INN

Above, one of the public houses photographed, by or for, John Minns dating this view (like most others from his collection) to around 1901/1902. An advert for the Carlisle Old Brewery can be made out and they obviously supplied the beer, however at some time after 1902 the pub was sold to the Maryport Brewery Co. Behind is the chimney of Carr's Biscuit Factory and it was this firm that demolished the Plough around 1954/55.

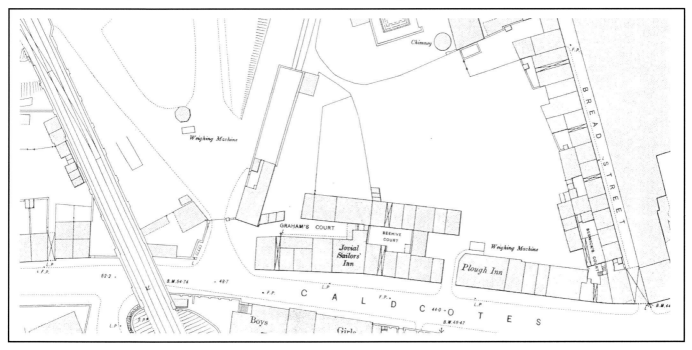

The 1899 O.S. map showing the location of the Plough and also the original Jovial Sailor, note Carr's chimney marked on the map. Bee Hive court was named after a pub of that name that stood there around 1840.

PLOUGH INN

As stated Carr's demolished the Plough around 1955, however they gave a history of this property in their works magazine known as the *Topper Off* and from this article dating to the Summer of 1955, the following is reproduced.

Photo: D. C. Small

The Old Plough

The demolition of the "Old Plough" has aroused the interest of many people in the history of this old building which for so long has been a familiar feature of our frontage. The extract quoted below from an article in our May 1935 issue written by Mr. J. T. Coulthard, a former warehouse manager, answers some of the questions which are being asked. — Ed.

WHEN this house was erected about one hundred and fifty years ago, it was an ordinary farmstead, Caldcotes Farm, and the licence was not obtained until fifty years later. Extensive agricultural operations were carried on here. Fields down to the river Eden, and where Holy Trinity Church now stands, and from Broad Guards on the eastern side of Caldewgate to beyond Silloth Street were farmed by the owner occupier of the farm house, Mr. Lister.

Lister's Well

When he sold the field across the way to the Ecclesiastical Commissioners to build Holy Trinity Church, there was a well in it from which the local residents drew their supplies. Water continued to be drawn from it when the field on the high side was being used as a burial ground. The only alternative supply was water from the river Eden hawked through the streets and sold for a few pence per pail. A condition was enforced that if this well was ever covered over,

26

a pump must be erected to mark the place. In a little recess in the Trinity school wall the pump still stands to mark the site of "Lister's Well."

Quoits a hundred years ago

The farm became the property of Mr. James McCutcheon and when he obtained the licence for this house he gave it a name suggesting an agricultural connection. But the activities of the Plough Inn developed in another direction. In its grounds there was a well-known quoiting alley. This game seems to have been very popular in Carlisle and the neighbourhood about one hundred years ago. In 1830 five hundred people assembled to play or witness the competition in the Crown Inn gardens which extended down to Collier Lane. Substantial prizes were offered at these contests. The game was played with iron rings weighing about 7-lbs. These had to be pitched about twenty-one yards to a target fixed in the ground. Enthusiasts liked to hear the metallic ring of the quoit when one dropped on top of another thrown by a competitor especially near the more. The game is still played in the south of Scotland.

Cock Fighting in the Plough Yard

In an uncovered building in the Plough Yard many a battle has been fought to a finish with local game cocks. For many years cockfighting as a sport had a large following. Carlisle had a central cockpit in Lowther Street. Many of the public schools encouraged it "to harden the feelings of those about to enter the army" as one writer suggests, and many birds were reared in the country districts for competitive purposes. The men from Burgh would accept the challenge of the Dalstoners with their "Black Reds" and on these occasions groups of men from the surrounding countryside were attracted to the Plough Yard to witness these exhibitions. Excitement round the ring was often keen while the sentry on the low roofed building was watching for the "Bobby" coming along Caldewgate. With the mauling of the birds by a sharp pointed spur fixed to their feet and legs, the law had to intervene, and although a few may in some lonely place outwit the police, it is a sport practically extinct.

From the above article (originally written in 1935) it would seem then that the property was built around 1785 and what was then Caldcotes Farm became the Plough public house around 1835. The only snag with this date is that the Carlisle trade directories of the time do not list the Plough until as late as 1852. A likely explanation for this late date is that prior to 1852 the pub carried a beer house licence, trade directories and maps tended not to name properties that did not carry a Full licence though they often give a separate list of beer sellers/beer houses, these consist of a list of surnames and address. In trying to pin down an earlier date for the Plough we need to refer to the earlier Carlisle directories and their lists of beer sellers/beer houses, these seem to indicate that between 1837-44 there were two pubs in Caldcotes and these can be identified as the 'Sailor' which got a Full licence by 1840 and the Bee Hive which was a beer house. However, the 1847 directory lists a second beer house by that date and it is suggested that this is the Plough and about the date when it first opened.

The Plough must have done a good trade at least in later years as it is recorded that in just one month (July 1913) the Maryport Brewery supplied 29 barrels of ale and 3 barrels of stout.

JOINERS ARMS

An undated photo but circa 1907 is probably not far off the mark. James Turner took over the licence on the 6 December 1897 and held it until at least 1912. The pub was a tied house being the property of Iredale's brewery in1894, that this brewery owned the pub is surprising considering that Graham's Queens brewery stood just a few yards away to the right.

A few of the Carlisle pubs are known to have carried nicknames and even at the time of writing some people still refer to the Joiners as 'Blue-Lugs'. This name is thought to have originated during the State Management years, it seems that during the 1930's a manager had blue- veined ears and became known to his customers by this nickname. However, an earlier alternative explanation for this name is that the pub was so called because some of it's customers were from the nearby Creighton's saw mill and timber yard, these men used blue- coloured pencils for marking out timber to be cut and were in the habit of keeping these pencils behind their ears.

The Joiners Arms along with the Kings Head in Fisher Street and the Sportsman can claim to be one of the oldest surviving Carlisle pubs. The *Cumberland Pacquet* newspaper carried an advert for the sale of the Joiners which was to take place on the 20 September 1785, at this time the property was owned by Mrs Mary Donald who according to the newspaper along with her late husband David Donald had owned the property 'for upwards of forty years'. In fact I have been informed that much of the structure of today's Joiners Arms is the original 18th century brickwork though modern rendering conceals evidence of its true age, having said that there has been one definite structural alteration to the pub at some time in its history and this can be seen in the above photo. I refer here to a later roof that has been added, the line of where the original 18th century roof once was can be made out on the front chimney stack, this means the pub has been enlarged from what was once a smaller property.

ROYAL OAK

Above: the Royal Oak then an off license when this view was taken sometime between 1955-60. The opening to the left was the entrance to Studholmes Lane, (see map below).

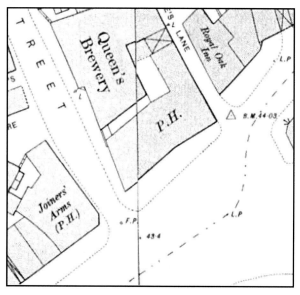

Above, detail from the 1899 OS map

This old Caldewgate pub very likely had its origins back in the 18th century but the earliest reference found to date, is to a rather dramatic incident during 1821 when it was reported in the *Carlisle Journal* that a Mr Anderson, who was a surgeon, was shot at in Caldewgate near the Royal Oak. It seems that this was an attempted robbery and the discharging of the firearm was to frighten him into given up his money.By the 1890's the Royal Oak was owned by the Carlisle New Brewery but when the State Management took over it ceased trading as a public house and by 1920 had become an off licence This it remained until 1987 when as a 'Cellar 5' off sales it was sold to Graham & Bowness who had it demolished for an extension to their garage.

WILLIAM JAMES M.P.

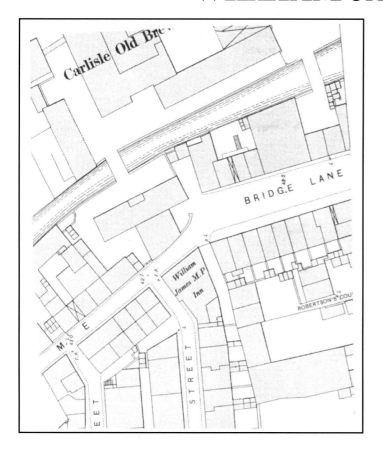

In a list of inns upon which billets were issued for the Yeomanry Cavalry on their arrival at Carlisle was that known by the sign of the "William James, M.P." It used to be more familiarly called "the Billy James." I had an inquiry about it a fortnight ago, and another seeker of information has been sounding the deep well of the local knowledge of Mr. Sam Jordan, who writes as follows:—"In response to the query put by 'Citizen' as to how, or when, the William James, M.P., public-house, in Willow Holme, got its name I know nothing. But in beating about the bush a bit I learn from an old residenter or two, and given in their own twang, 'It was when Billy James, of Barrock Lodge, was first elected member of Parliament for Carel, and when the sign was hoisted the house was kept by William Rigg, better known as Billy the Piper, a pipe maker by trade, as the name implies, and as local tattle goes, 'a reet decent fellow he was,' and respected by everybody, but he did a lot o' mischief wid the stuff that he dabbled in.'" Mr. William James was first returned for Carlisle in 1820 in succession to Mr. Curwen, after a severe contest with Sir Philip Musgrave. He was an advanced Radical at that time, but some forty years later he grew timid and modified some of the political views which had commended him to the electors in his earlier days. That election of 1820 was not the one at which the riots took place in Shaddongate. It was in 1826 that Sir Philip Musgrave was put upon a loom and threatened with a ducking in the mill dam.

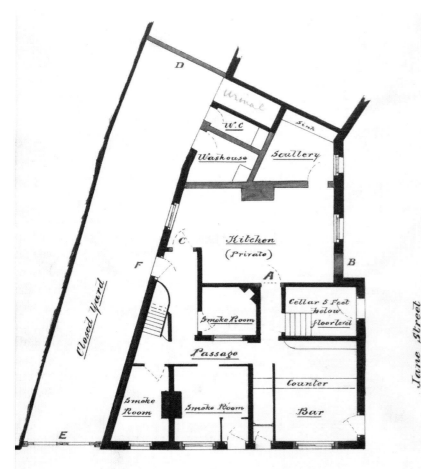

Above, some Carlisle pubs were even arousing interest during the Victorian age. This article appeared in the *Carlisle Journal* of the 9 June 1896 and goes someway in explaining why the pub acquired it's name.

This pub is the only property appearing in the book which is not accompanied by an illustration. However, being curiously named ,little known and sufficient detail (including the 1898 plan, left) having been found whilst researching this book, it deserves inclusion in this survey of the city's pubs in 1894.

The 'William James' was located at the junction of Jane Street and Willow Holme (see 1899 O.S map top left). The age of the property is unknown but it started trading as a beerhouse between 1834-37 and as indicated in the newspaper article the first licensee was William Rigg. Regarding the naming of the pub, it would seem that in his early political career William James was classed as a 'Radical'(i.e. having advanced liberal views or put another way he would have supported or been active in trying to achieve better conditions for the working class.). As a result he would have been held in high regard by Caldewgate residents many of whom were weavers who suffered particular hardship and the naming of this pub after him reflected his popularity. By the 1890's it was owned by the Carlisle New Brewery but by the Edwardian period the pub was targeted for closure by the city's licensing magistrates and despite a petition signed by 150 locals who wanted the pub retained it was closed in 1912.

WAGON AND HORSES

Opposite the Old Brewery, between Milbourne street on the left and Brewery Row on the right, stood the Waggon and Horses Inn. The above photo is from the Minn's collection of Carlisle pubs, but this is one of five that does not seem to have been taken at the usual date of about 1902. The reason for this doubt is that the name on the licensing board gives Noble Harding and as he was publican of the 'Waggon' from 4.6.1894 to 19.11.1897, then the photo above very likely dates to some time between this period. Further evidence that backs up the above photo being earlier than most others from the Minns collection is the barber's pole that can just be made out in the bottom right of the photo. This was attached to 18 Brewery Row and in 1894 W. Harding (there seems to be a family connection here), a hairdresser, occupied this property but it closed sometime pre-1900.

The building date of this pub is unknown but it must be pre - 1796 as this is when the property acquired its licence. Whether it was called the Waggon and Horses at this date is uncertain but by 1822 it was trading under that name. Note the rather bare exterior of the pub in respect to a pictorial signboard. Indeed absence of advertising of this kind is apparent on many of the late Victorian pub photos seen in this book. It seems that this was not always the case as there is evidence that at some time pre-1894 their use had been more common, as in an article entitled 'Celebrated inn signs in Carlisle', which appeared in the Carlisle Journal 9.1.1894, a Carlisle born correspondent, then living in Glasgow, stated that he 'remembered many old signs' that were once on Carlisle's pubs and said some were 'works of art' and went on to list 'the Waggon and Horses, Lion and Lamb, Black Swan, Green Man, White Lion, Hound and Otter (this painted by the late John Dobson) and the Saracen's Head'. The 'Waggon' was closed by the State in 1917 and demolished in 1924 to make way for the widening of Caldew Bridge.

MALTSTERS ARMS

The name of Robert.G Pattinson can be made out on the sign board, meaning that this photograph was taken on or after 2 June 1902, this being the date that he took over the licence. This is another pub that did not have a pictorial sign though as can be seen there was an illuminated gas lit star, a type of decoration short lived because it can be linked to celebrations for the coronation of King Edward VII . The pub was not affected by the incoming State scheme but the exterior was altered by them in more recent times.

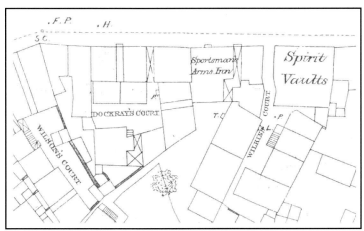

Left, the 1865 O.S map for the John Street area of Caldewgate. The 'Maltsters' at this date is marked as a 'Spirit Vault.' This means it was then in occupation by a wine and spirit merchant. This implies that the property was an off licence shop or store, which was not the case. During the 19th century it was quite common for wine and spirit merchants to open as a public house whilst conducting their other profession in the same building. There is however an odd fact about some of the Victorian Carlisle pubs that had spells of tenancy or ownership by wine and spirit merchants in that, quite often, they would not display a pub name, as here in 1865, or drop an existing name when they took occupation of a pub, as with the 'Bricklayers Arms,' when J.H.Wilson took over. These pubs that did not carry a typical name or sign but just gave that of the licensees surname, perhaps with 'Vaults' stuck on the end, can be classed as 'Board Inns'.

As a licensed house, what was to become the 'Maltsters', can be traced back to 1857, when a John Wilkin was listed as a wine and spirit merchant at, what was then, 32 John Street (his name was remembered in the alleyway Wilkins Court see map above). However, it was not until as late as 1880 that the pub acquired the title of the Maltsters Arms. During the 1890's the pub was owned by the Carlisle New Brewery Co. The pub was closed and demolished in 2004.

BRICKLAYERS ARMS

Almost next door to the Maltsters Arms Inn stood the Bricklayers Arms (see 1899 O.S. map below). Judging from the exterior appearance of this property, i.e. sandstone tiled roof and the crude timber purlings that had not been cut by a saw (these were exposed during demolition), suggests a date of construction to some time in the 18th century, though there is at the time of writing no documentary records found to back this up.

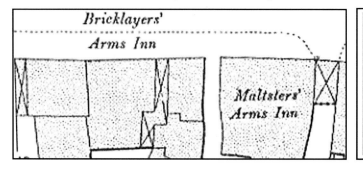

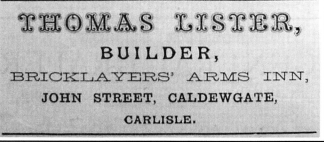

The earliest record found to it as a pub does not occur until 1847, when J.Gallery had a beer house licence, although it is not named. This situation changes in 1852 when the pub is listed as the Weavers Arms, 34 John Street, still managed by J. Gallery. This it remained until circa 1863 then it had a name change to the Sportsman's Arms Inn. However yet another name change circa 1882 finally resulted in the Bricklayers' Arms. The 1894 register shows a Thomas Lister as the owner of this property. He is known to have been a bricklayer and builder by trade, so this explains the naming of the pub. It seems the pub remained privately owned by Mr Lister and John Hind Wilson, whose name appears on the photo, took over the tenancy on the 3 June 1901. Mr Wilson was a wine and spirit merchant and also a beer bottler who ran a successful business, not just from this pub, but also from the Wheatsheaf in Rickergate, which he owned. This name in the Carlisle drinks trade came to an end in 1911 with Mr Wilson's death. The final tenant of the Bricklayers was R.Lowry *(1912-16) who continued to bottle beer and spirits albeit on a smaller scale, but the incoming State scheme judged the pub unsuitable for its new plans and closed it on the 12 July 1916. The building stood for many more years though, and the property was not finally pulled down until 2001. *See green glass beer bottle on page 137.

LORNE ARMS INN

The Lorne Arms was a corner property standing at the junction of Broadguards and Shaddongate (see map on next page) and it was owned by the Carlisle Old Brewery Co. John Skelton took over the licence on the 4 March 1901 so the photo was taken on or after this date, but as it comes from the Minns collection it almost certainly dates no later than 1903. In the window are posters which advertise Samuel Cody appearing in *Klondyke Nugget* which are misleading as this was performed in the city in 1899 and it seems they were used long after the event to attract customers attention to the window display.

 The name 'Lorne Arms' is linked to Princess Louise's visit to Carlisle in 1877. She had married the Marquis of Lorne and came to Carlisle principally to open the new Victoria Viaduct. *Slater's Directoy*, 1879, lists the Lorne Arms at 30 Shaddongate but a rare copy of *Arthur's Carlisle Directory* (which appears to date to 1878) lists the pub at this address under a different name, the Weavers Arms. The evidence then from these directories shows that a name change had taken place and that the Lorne Arms was formerly the Weavers.

 The history of this Shaddongate property as the Weavers Arms can be traced back to 1837 (the pub is not marked on the 1865 O.S map because it seems to have been relegated back down to a beerhouse at this time) and was owned or tenanted by a Thomas Jackson for nearly 30 years, the trail of the pub disappears from the records pre 1837.

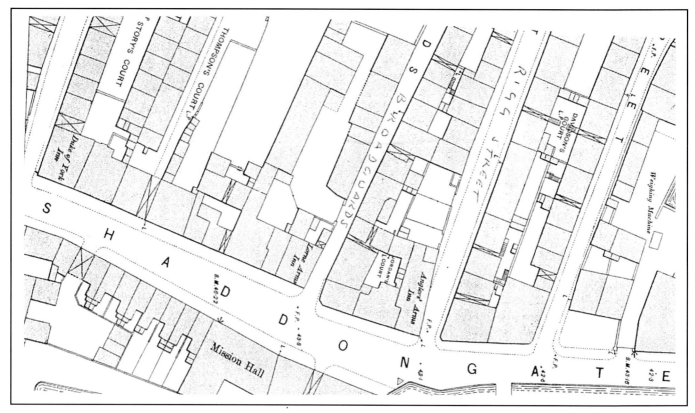

Above, the 1899 O.S map for the Shaddongate area showing from left to right, the Duke of York, Lorne Arms and the Anglers Arms.

As T. Jackson is listed as a beer seller in 1837, it looks like the history of this property as a pub is closely linked to the 'beer house boom' that took place all over Britain due to the Duke of Wellington's Act of 1830, which allowed any householder to set up a pub (albeit just to serve beer) for the sum of 2 guineas, which bought him a licence. This law broke down barriers as up to that time the sale of alcoholic beverages had been strictly controlled by licensing magistrates. As a result of this act beer houses rapidly increased throughout Britain from 24,000 in 1830 to 46,000 in 1836 and the Weavers Arms likely owes its origins to this act. Indeed the evidence for a mini 'boom' in Carlisle pubs because of the 1830 legislation can be seen on a study of the earlier Carlisle directories, particularly that of 1837.

Dating or attempting to date the building of the properties covered by this publication is often the most difficult when discussing the individual history of a Carlisle pub. Considering the Lorne/Weavers Arms there is nothing definite known as to when this property was built. One possible guide, however, could be the date when some of the housing in BroadGuards went up, this being 1804/05. However, as the pub fronted Shaddongate, the building is likely to be somewhat earlier. Interestingly there is an historical reference to the Shaddongate area that could be relevant to the other two licensed properties that appear in the above map.

This is an advert in the *Cumberland Pacquet* for 1797; it states 'A newly built dwelling house situated in Shaddongate occupied by William Gibson as a public house.' Unfortunately this fails to name the pub but at least it indicates that a licensed property was already established in Shaddongate in the late 18th century. The earliest record of a **named** pub in this area is in the licensing register for 1822 which lists a property called the Minerva the publican being a James Rennison. There is **no** link between the Minerva and Weavers Arms. This was a separate and second public house trading in Shaddongate from at least 1822-1855, then it disappears. The following directory however, for 1858, lists the Anglers Inn and I would suggest that this had been formerly called the Minerva.

VALUABLE FREEHOLD PROPERTY IN SHADDON-GATE AND DUKE STREET, CARLISLE, FOR SALE, IN LOTS, OR AS A WHOLE, TO SUIT PURCHASERS.

MESSRS. R. HARRISON and SON beg to announce that they have received instructions to OFFER for SALE, at the BUSH HOTEL, on TUESDAY, APRIL 30th, at 7 p.m., all that Old-Established WINE and SPIRIT SHOP, with HOUSE attached, being No. 48, SHADDONGATE and Corner of DUKE STREET, so successfully carried on for upwards of the last 70 years by the present owner, Mr. Jonathan Story, and his Father ; TWO SHOPS, with Rooms behind and over, being Nos. 44 and 46, SHADDONGATE ; THREE COTTAGES, situate in and being Nos. 46 and 48, DUKE STREET ; TWO COTTAGES, with flat over same, situate in and being Nos. 8 and 10, STORY'S COURT, DUKE STREET ; and FIVE COTTAGES in STORY'S COURT, DUKE STREET, with Out-offices and Open Spaces. The Property, No. 48, Shaddongate, being situated in a dense and populous neighbourhood, and close to the chief Factories and Mills, is one of the best sites in the whole of Carlisle for a Tavern, and under active management can not fail to prove a lucrative business.

The Two Shops and Ten Cottages yield a gross annual rent of £95 15s.

Above, sales advert dating to 1895 for 48 Shaddongate, then known as Story's Vaults.
A year later the first record to it being named the Duke of York appears.

DUKE OF YORK

This undated photo is believed to have been taken in 1900 at the time of the celebrations for the relief of Ladysmith, or Mafeking, during the Boer war.

Note the pictorial sign board depicting the Duke of York. However, the naming of this pub and its earlier history is not very clear, as there is no record of this property being called the Duke of York pre -1896.

Referred to as 'Story's Vaults' in 1895, the property was put up for sale (see advert, previous page) on the 26th of April of that year and was purchased by the Carlisle New Brewery. Prior to this, as indicated in the advert, the property had been owned by a family called Story who traded as wine and spirit merchants. There is enough evidence from the licensing registers to show that they were also running the premises as a public house. As indicated by the advert the Story's had a long connection with the building and this is confirmed by the licensing register for 1823 which names Jonathan and George Story as licensees, the pub then being called the 'Board' (i.e. a pub without a proper name or sign). Instead what would have been displayed would have been the licensee's surname put up on the front of the pub on a **board**. 'Board Inns' are usually the result of the pub being occupied by a wine and spirit merchant who quite frequently it seems were reluctant to give their pub a proper title or sign, or display its original name when they took over an existing pub.

From the surviving records then, it seems certain that the pub was not called the Duke of York during the 70 - year period of the Story's ownership and it looks like it was the brewery who first named the pub, this taking place as late as 1896. Yet to conflict with the 1896 naming theory is the presence of Duke Street. This street name can be traced back to at least 1842, which suggests that the pub could have carried the name Duke of York at some stage in its earlier history and its one-time presence was remembered in the street name. For this earlier naming to be possible the property would have to have been a pub pre the 1823 register which called it the 'Board'. This can not be ruled out as the house is certainly old enough and could even be a candidate for the unidentified pub sited in Shaddongate in 1797. The publican's name, Riddell, can be seen on the photo and he was licensee here from the 1.3.1897 up to the 4.3.1901.

MILBOURNE ARMS

The Milbourne Arms seen here circa 1901 was constructed in 1852. The pub was named after the family who lived at Denton Foot and owned the land on which these buildings stood. It soon acquired a full licence as it is first recorded in *Slater's Directory*, 1855 . By 1894 it was the property of the New Brewery and George Edmondson was their manager. However it was not a good year for him as the licensed register book put a black mark against him for supplying liquor to a constable while on duty and Edmondson was fined 10 shillings and sixpence.

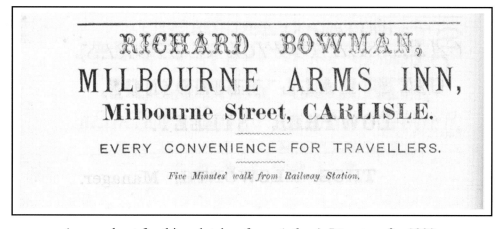

A rare advert for this pub taken from *Arthur's Directory* for 1880.

WOOLPACK INN

An undated view of the Wool Pack Inn, Milbourne Street. The dress of the little girl in the doorway suggests a date of circa 1925 but there is another clue in the photo that indicates an earlier period perhaps pre - State Management, namely the display of drink related advertising and what appear to be spirit or beer bottles in the window. This is not consistent with the State Scheme's crusade of removing advertising that promoted the sale of intoxicating liquors in those houses that were to remain open. A State Management report dated 1916, said 'the display of bottles in the windows is also being abandoned and it is hoped that in the course of time no adventitious aid will be given to the sale of intoxicants in the city'. This action must have been carried out quickly and thoroughly, if a report dated 31 December 1918 is to be believed. The report was entitled '*Effects on appearance of Carlisle streets*'. The following is an extract from it: ' All bottles have been removed from the windows which are now draped with plain curtains'.

What can be said for certain about dating the above photo is that it must be after 1911 as this was when J. Ellwood took over as manager and his name can be made out on the original photo that was used for this book. But, when was the property built and when was the first reference to the 'Woolpack'? The answer to the first question is *after 1865* , as it does not appear on the Carlisle Ordnance Survey for that year. It was, however, probably built by 1869 as there is an unnamed beerhouse listed in the street. The first definite reference to the pub comes in the Carlisle street directory for 1873. Again the beerhouse is not named, but this time an address, 83 Milbourne Street is given. Although the street numbering sometimes changed elsewhere in the city, 83 Milbourne Street is confirmed as the Woolpack in the 1875 licensing register and in a later directory.

Of the three pubs in Milbourne street in 1894 the Woolpack had the shortest history. One of its rivals namely the Spinners Arms (this property still stands on the same side as the Woolpack but further up the street) was somewhat older and it seems to have been one of the first properties built on that side. It was put up between 1846-1853 and named by 1858. The Spinners was owned by the Maryport Brewery but was not required by the incoming State scheme and they closed it.

Returning to the Woolpack, at 1898 it was owned by the Carlisle New Brewery Co.

PRINCE OF WALES

Above, this is one of the Carlisle pub photos that was taken by or for John Minns and like most others it dates to around 1901/02.That the view is post 1900 is confirmed by what appear to be tram line wires which can just be made out in the top right hand corner of the photo. The property itself was built after 1853 and the earliest reference to the Prince of Wales is on the 1865 O.S map. There was a bowling green located at the rear,though whether it was in use after 1890 is not known. John Reay acquired the licence and a long lease on behalf of the Carlisle New Brewery about 1892.

Left, the label dates between 1897 - 1907. Along with T&J Minns, John Reay was the most successful of Carlisle's late Victorian licensed victuallers as he owned public house properties and in the 1890's Reay was also a major shareholder in the Carlisle New Brewery Co .Mr Reay started out in the licensing trade in Liverpool, he came to Carlisle in the late 1870's and managed a number of the city's pubs, some ten years later he had actually achieved the ownership of the Gaol Tap. Quite a number of old bottles survive carrying Reays name though he seems to have concentrated more on bottling whisky than beer.

This label is printed in its original colour on the back cover, also see bottle on page 140.

NELSON BRIDGE

Left, the property is seen here about 1974. It had closed three years earlier, just after the State scheme had ended. What became the pub and the short stretch of terraced housing it was attached to were built between 1866-72 (i.e. the block between the railway lines and Elm Street, see map below). The terrace had been slightly longer but the laying in of the new railway goods line in 1877 required the demolition of two properties at that end of the block. In 1873 the property was a grocer's shop but it was listed as the 'Nelson Bridge' two years later.

The property seen above was not the first public house to carry the name Nelson Bridge. There had been an earlier and somewhat larger building of this name which stood virtually opposite at the junction of Denton Street and Charlotte Street. This Nelson Bridge Hotel is marked on the 1865 O.S map and had been built there circa 1856. It took its name from the bridge that was built in 1852 to link Denton Holme and the city centre.

However, when a new railway freight line was laid along the West bank of the River Caldew, (i.e. Denton Holme side in 1876/77 see arrow on 1899 map) the old bridge had to be raised and this meant that the approach roads from Charlotte Street and Denton Street had to be ramped and slightly realigned. The old 'Nelson Bridge' was in the way of these alterations and was pulled down by 1877, however it must have been abandoned and awaiting demolition for around a year or two as we know that the licence had been transferred to the smaller Elm Street property opposite about 1874/75.

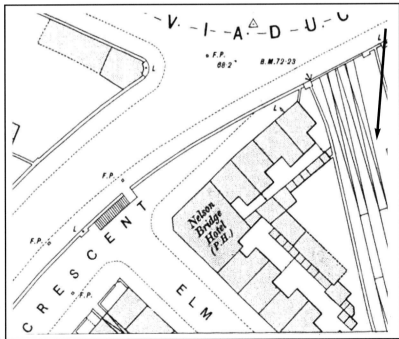

This second 'Nelson Bridge' traded as a pub for nearly a century but little of note seems to have been recorded about it, how it ever came to be classed as a hotel defies explanation as it must have been one of Carlisle's smallest public houses. It is known that many of its customers were railwaymen and the pub was actually owned by the Citadel Joint Station Committee.

PUBS OF THE WAPPING
A SUB DISTRICT OF BOTCHERGATE

The name 'Wapping' is still used by a few people today when referring to the Crown/James Street area, but in reality the name and the memory of this one-time industrial part of Carlisle and the community that went with it is fast fading away. The map below illustrates the whole block of what was once known as 'Wapping'. This was not its official name, as it was part of the parish of St Stephens, but a slang name linked to the beatling of cloth, a process that was used during the 18th century in the textile industry.It is known that there was a stampery located in this area as early as the 1750's, but by the 1820's technical improvements in the industry made this 'Wapping' of cloth redundant. However, as some of the housing and industry was going up in this area during the early 19th century this old name stuck and continued to be used well into the 20th century in referring to this district.

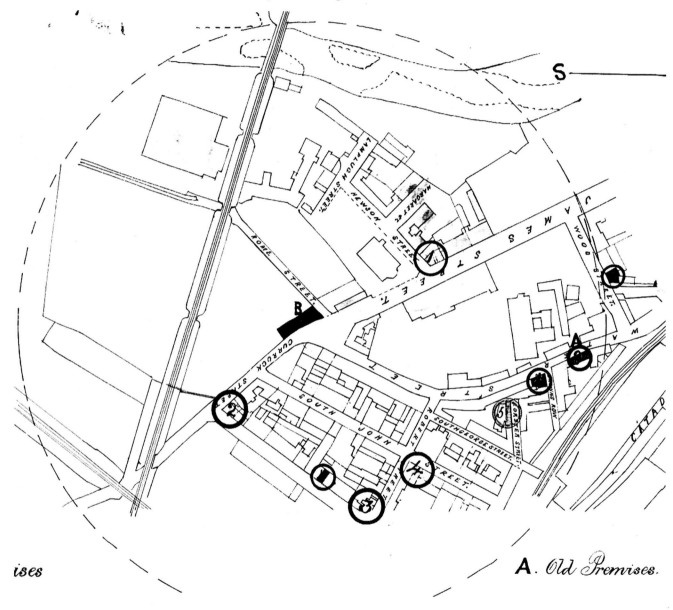

MAP OF THE WAPPING AREA SHOWING THE LOCATION OF ITS PUBS CIRCA 1872

The properties marked by the larger circles and numbered **1** and **3** remained open for trade into the1930's. These are the LNWR.Inn and GOLIATH, property **2** was the ODDFELLOWS INN which closed during 1916 and **4** was the MASONS ARMS, but this closed in 1908. Those indicated by smaller circles were all closed between 1873-93. Starting in Wood St, this pub was called the Jovial Hatter, next is the property marked **A** this indicates the site of Iredales original High Brewery and Cumberland Wrestlers before the demolition which brought about the move to the site marked **B**. Next down was a pub called the Pack Horse sited in Browns Row, then a pub marked **5** called the Carters Arms and finally into Crown Street where the beer house known as the Half Moon, (just down from the Goliath), was located.

LONDON & NORTH WESTERN RAILWAY INN

The above drawing and plan below are from an auction catalogue and shows the pub in 1898 and it was bought by the Carlisle Old Brewery Co at that sale. The L&.N W Railway Inn stood on the corner of what was Hewson Street and

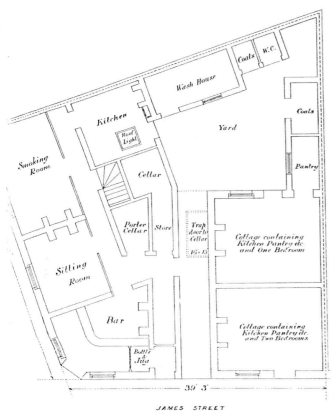

James Street, the property itself was built sometime between 1843 and 1853. The first indication to the building as a pub is in 1861 when Joshua Robinson is listed as a beer retailer in James street. It is not marked on the 1865 O S map but this is because it was a beer house. Then in Slater's Directory of 1869 it is listed as the 'St Stephen's Inn', so called because of the presence of the nearby church of that name. However, this name was either unpopular or, more likely, there were complaints from the clergy about a public house being associated with a church, so the name was dropped and around 1875 it became known as the 'London & North Western Railway Inn'. This railway company was in charge of the London to Carlisle main line and no doubt some of its employees were patrons of this pub. In the late 1870's Halls Crown Brewery supplied the beer but it is not clear whether they owned the property, then, as mentioned above, it was put up for sale in 1898. The Carlisle Old Brewery Co. then owned it up to the arrival of the State in 1916, but it was not closed straightaway and remained open until the 2.10.1938, when it was shut so that trade could be transferred to Redferns' newly opened Cumberland Wrestlers.

CUMBERLAND WRESTLERS

Another photo with nothing to date it but close study of the later Carlisle street directories suggests a 1897-1901 date when John Miller had the licence and it is presumably him standing in the doorway. Before this date the manager was a W. Chambers.

The property was built in late 1875 or early 1876 and was the second pub to carry this name in the Wapping area. The first Wrestlers was attached to Iredales earlier High Brewery located in Water Street but, as referred to previously, all this block had to be demolished to make way for the Citadel Station extension. However, Iredale experienced some difficulty in getting a licence for his new Cumberland Wrestlers during 1876. This seems to have been caused by some confusion between the magistrates and Iredale, they believed he had received and agreed to compensation for the loss of his licence at his original site and in doing so had surrendered the said licence. This in fact was not the case and he had gone ahead oblivious of this and had the new pub built thinking that he could just transfer the license from the old property to the new Wrestlers. So, it came as a shock when the magistrates refused to grant a licence.

Iredale and his solicitor then had to present a court case to overturn the earlier decision. Underlying this apparent confusion though was the real issue of the hard-line attitude and outright reluctance by the Carlisle licensing magistrates to grant new licenses anywhere in the city from 1870 onwards. To convince the magistrates that there was a need for his new pub the solicitor pointed out that four public houses had been done away within the area. Two had been pulled down, the Pack Horse and the Carters Arms, around 1874, the Half Moon had been closed and the old Cumberland Wrestlers was about to be pulled down. The existing rival pubs were described as 'all more or less tap shops, possessing no accommodation at all, except for very poor travellers and in fact were merely places for the sale and consumption of spirituous liquors.' Whereas they said that Iredale's new pub was 'by far the best in the neighbourhood having ample accommodation for travellers.' The line of thinking here seems to have been the belief that the new Citadel station would have a westwards exit into this area and that passengers getting out on that side would find it the only inn with spacious modern accommodation. It was also believed that houses would be shortly built on Bousteads Grassing so increasing the demand for drink in the area. As it turned out neither of these speculations turned into reality, though houses were eventually built on the Grassing albeit some 45 years later.

The evidence must have been persuasive as the new Cumberland Wrestlers got its licence in the October of 1876. Interestingly, in Iredale's first application for a license for his new property he wanted to call it the 'Royal Hotel' no doubt in an attempt to 'dress it up' to get it past the magistrates. Iredale's Wrestlers survived until 1937 when it was pulled down and replaced by today's Redfern designed pub that stands on the same spot.

ODDFELLOWS INN

Delivery day at the OddFellows Inn about 1901. This pub stood on the corner of Crown Street and Currock Street and by this date was either owned or supplied with beer by the Maryport Brewery Co. In 1894 its beer came from Hall's Crown Street brewery and it was owned by Harrison Hall. Though he lived in Liverpool there was a link between him and the Carlisle brewery of that name and it is the only property known to have been owned by them. In 1911 the Maryport Brewery definitely supplied the beer, as from one of their surviving sales /delivery ledgers we get the following information; Jan - June 1911 the pub received 159 barrels of ale, 16 kilderkins of I.P.B and 47 kilderkins of Stout. Other than the entry for Stout it is not clear what the other 2 beer types are, however after consulting an original document relating to the nearby Masons Arms we find; (see below).

1905	Mild	$220\frac{1}{2}$	34/-	2d. to 3d.
	Bitter..	25	40/-	3d. to 4d.

This then almost certainly provides the answer. Dated 1905 it shows 220 barrels of Mild against just 25 of Bitter. The Maryport Brewery figures show a similar marked difference, with 159 barrels of what must be Mild Ale against just 16 kilderkins of what must stand for India Pale Beer/Bitter. There is a significant difference in the popularity between the two beer types presumably explained by the Bitter being up to twopence dearer and it has to be remembered that money supply would have been tight in this area, even so Mild was still the popular drink in Carlisle even into the 1950's.

Finally when was the Oddfellows built? It must have been after 1853 as it is not shown on Asquith's Carlisle street map, it is recorded as a beer house though in Slater's Directory of 1855 so it must have been just newly opened by that date, then in 1858 it is listed as the Oddfellows having obtained a full licence. Years later it was deemed unsuitable by the State Management and it was closed on the 11 October 1916.

GOLIATH INN

The view above of the Goliath dates to about 1901/02. The pub was located at the corner of Crown and Robert Street (see map on p 52). The property itself was built between 1842-1848 and it quickly became a public house as it is listed in the Carlisle street directory for 1852. The pub was named after a freight locomotive that ran on the Newcastle and Carlisle railway from 1836 until it was broken up in 1864. Note the unusual spelling of the name as GOLIAH. It seems that this was not a spelling error and it could be that the steam engine carried the name spelt this way. The Maryport Brewery Co bought the pub during 1892 and it did a good trade judging by the brewery's delivery ledger of 1911. By then a James Hewitt was licensee and between January and June of that year the pub received 175 barrels of Mild ale, 17 kilderkins of India Pale beer and 31 kilderkins of Stout. When the State took over in 1916 it was not closed and by 1917 it was advertised as a 'Special Food Tavern.' Drink was still available but now more rationed and controlled than the earlier years. The pub was closed in 1938.

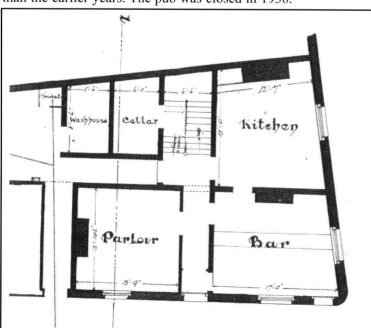

Left is a plan view of the Goliath's interior as it looked in 1898.

For a pub that did a large trade then the bar room was rather on the small side, presumably the Parlour was part of the pub accommodation to cater for busy periods. There were plans to enlarge the bar and exterior windows at this time, but it appears these alterations did not go ahead until December 1916. The premises of Carlisle Glass now occupy the site of the Goliath.

MASONS ARMS

Above, the right hand side of South John Street and what had been the Masons Arms. Part of the Citadel railway station dominates the background and some of this street would have been demolished to make way for it. This photo is undated but is thought to have been taken around 1956-58. Construction of these houses occurred at sometime between 1822-1842, and the first reference to it named as the 'Masons Arms' is in 1847, when a Thomas Todd was the licence holder and his association with the pub was remembered in Todd's Court as indicated on the O.S. map of 1899. The choice of name for this pub could be linked to it being frequented in these early years by workers from Thomas Nelson's marble works, which was located near to Crown Street in the 1840's. The pub became a 'tied' house quite early, as it was bought by the Carlisle New Brewery Co in 1880. Between 1902-07 the pub sold on average four and half barrels a week, the bulk of which was Mild Ale. This doesn't sound much but one barrel contains 36 Gallons or, put another way 288 pints and considering the competition in this area from other pubs the Masons Arms seems to have done a good trade, however by the standards of the time this level of consumption may not have impressed the brewery owners as it was recorded in 1898 that the White Ox at St Nicholas 'sold **only** 5 or 6 barrels a week'. Whether or not there was any dissatisfaction with the beer sales at the Masons Arms this was not connected to its closure in 1908.

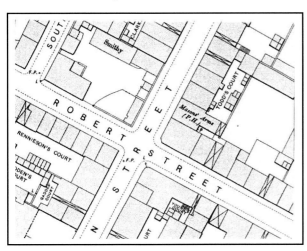

It was the refusal by the magistrates that year to renew its licence, explained by four somewhat standardised complaints used at the time to close pubs. These were 1. Premises badly ventilated and unsanitary, 2. Premises structurally deficient, 3. That the licence is unnecessary for the requirements of the area and 4. The police cannot properly supervise the premises. The New brewery put in a compensation claim for £2,170 and the pub was converted into a dwelling house.

BOTCHERGATE AREA

The following list covers all the public houses in this area in 1894. 'Wapping' and the London Road district come under this heading. The pubs doing the largest trade in this area at that time were the Caledonian, the original Cumberland (today's building dates to 1930), and the Crown. To a lesser extent the Golden Lion, Golden Fleece and the Samson also had a busy trade down that end of the town. Once again those pubs highlighted in bold are covered in more detail. The first six were located in Wapping and some of these are covered in previous pages.

1.	**LONDON & NORTH WESTERN**	CLOSED 1938
2.	**CUMBERLAND WRESTLERS**	PULLED DOWN 1937/38
3.	MOULDERS ARMS	CLOSED 25. 9. 1916/ HOUSE STILL STANDING
4.	**ODD FELLOWS**	CLOSED 11. 10. 1916
5.	**GOLIATH**	CLOSED 1938
6.	**MASONS ARMS**	CLOSED 1908
7.	**CROWN HOTEL**	STILL OPEN
8.	**QUEEN ADELAIDE**	CLOSED 1935
9.	**GOLDEN LION**	STILL OPEN
10.	**GOLDEN FLEECE**	NOW THE SOUTH END CLUB
11.	**WHITE OX**	CLOSED APRIL 1919
12.	RAILWAY HOTEL	STILL OPEN
13.	**SAMSON**	CLOSED 1917
14.	**EARL GREY**	PULLED DOWN CIRCA 1934
15.	**DEAKINS VAULTS**	CLOSED 1916
16.	ALBION	STILL OPEN
17.	**NORTHUMBERLAND ARMS**	CLOSED 12.7.1916
18.	HARE AND HOUNDS	CLOSED CIRCA 1924
19.	**ISMAYS VAULTS**	CLOSED CIRCA 1924
20.	CUMBERLAND	CLOSED 1929/30
21.	**RAILWAY TAVERN**	CLOSED CIRCA 1917
22.	**CALEDONIAN**	STILL OPEN

CROWN HOTEL

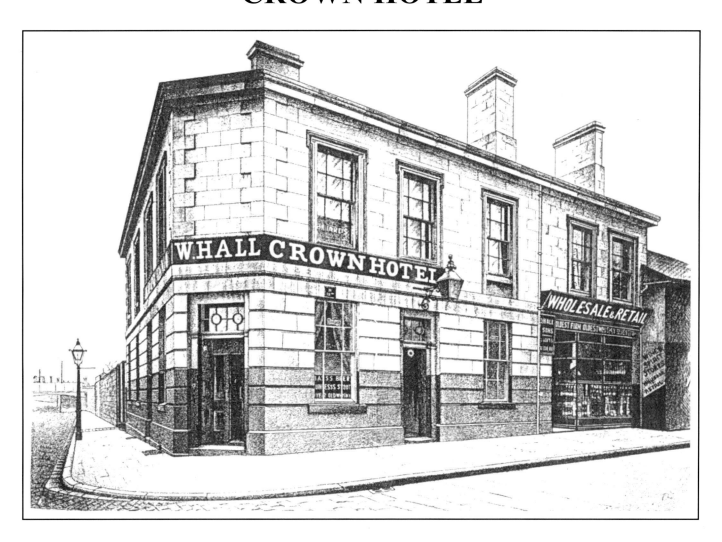

This view shows the pub in 1898 and is taken from a sales catalogue for that year. John Reay bought the 'Crown' at this sale for £11,400 and in turn leased it to the Carlisle New Brewery Co. This effectively brought about the end of a near 50-year association with the Hall family.

It seems there has been a pub called the Crown standing on this location since at least 1822 but it did not become a corner property until Crown Street was constructed between 1832- 41, prior to this there had been a solid building line and the cutting- in of the street to make a junction with Botchergate required the demolition of an existing property that adjoined the old Crown Inn.

Despite the early 19th century references to the Crown Inn it is unlikely that the building in the above illustration goes that far back. Close examination of maps indicate that pre -1865 it was a smaller property and it could be that the building in the above view was put up between 1854-64 replacing the earlier pub. The building appears to be constructed out of dressed stone blocks but this is misleading, as this is actually 'stucco' (a type of cement moulding) which has been applied over the brickwork to give the illusion of stone.

The Halls were associated with this site since circa 1850, in the capacity of tenants and managers. The owner of the pub though and an extensive block of land at its rear was C J Ferguson a Carlisle architect. The Halls made some use of the land at the rear of the Crown. The *Carlisle Journal* reported on the 21 April 1854 that there had been a large fireworks display. The same paper four years later reported that David Hall had organised a Cumberland Wrestling match 'the ground selected as the scene of this contest is the bowling green behind Mr Halls house.' Then in 1869 part of the land at the rear of the Crown was taken up by the construction of their brewery.

Lowingham Hall became the last member of the Hall family to hold the licence of the Crown. He was the eldest of David Hall's three sons and became a greyhound expert and reporter for *The Sportsman*. He was considered up to the time of his death (died at Baldwinholme on the 26 October 1928) one of the greatest authorities in Great Britain on greyhounds, he was also Chairman of the Carlisle and District Licensed Victuallers Association. At the 1898 sale of the Crown, he must have been quite determined to make the building the property of the family, as he actually bid up to £11,300 but failed in the attempt.

Above, the Crown is seen here sometime between 1903 - 1909 when D.J White held the licence. By this time the Carlisle New Brewery owned the pub. As in the previous illustration part of the pub was given over to a wine and spirit store.

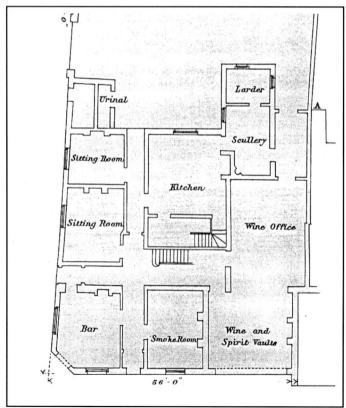

Left: plan of the internal lay-out of the Crown in 1898. Whereas the exterior of the present day Crown has seen little change from the views seen on this and the previous page the same can't be said for the interior. Writing in the Carlisle Journal in 1934 John Minns made a few comments about the pub as he remembered it during the late1870's, he said 'my earliest recollections of the Crown Hotel Botchergate was when it was kept by David Hall senior. This house was at that time much frequented by greyhound experts and fanciers, and pictures of many famous greyhounds, racehorses and jockeys adorned the walls of the rooms. No bars in those days'. This last comment must be a reference to the lack of a long bar and open plan layout, which of course can be found inside the present day Crown. Surprisingly even by the late 1890's the internal arrangement of the pub had not been modernised and as can be seen the older style of smoke rooms, sitting rooms (i.e. 'Snugs') had been retained. One last comment on the Crown site, which refers to a Roman relic. *The Carlisle Journal* 17 February 1899 reported the following 'gift to Tullie House museum from C J Ferguson, a statuette in white clay representing Venus, found when lowering the ground behind the hotel.'

QUEEN ADELAIDE

Above, bottom end of Botchergate about 1904, the position of the 'Queen Inn' is indicated by the arrow, note the 'Earl Grey' stood virtually opposite.

Left, a pencil drawing of the pub based on the above postcard view. The name 'Queen Inn' was painted on the front during the Edwardian period, however in 1894, records indicate that there was a large signboard on the pub, though whether this was pictorial or just painted letters is not known. The property was built sometime between 1822-1836 and it seems to owe its licensing origins to the 1830 Beerhouse Act. The first record for it is in 1837 when the street directory for that year lists a J Forster, beer seller, 'Queen Adelaide', 13 London Road (up until the 1860's this area was then part of London Road). The pub took its name from the wife of King William IV, she being a contemporary royal at the time the property acquired its license. By 1858 the name was dropped and the pub became the 'Queen Victoria Inn' then by the early 1870's it had become just the 'Queen Inn' and this name can just be made out on the circa 1904 postcard. The Carlisle New Brewery owned this pub from at least 1872 and in 1894 they appointed a John Robert Boone as the pub's new manager/tenant. J R Boone was allowed to bottle spirits for the carry-out trade and some old bottles can be found stamped with his and the pub's name. From this time there survives a list giving detail about the bar fittings. For example there were seven draw pumps (presumably this means 'beer engines) with about 40-60 feet of lead piping connecting these to the barrels in the cellar (the cellar was 7 feet deep). The pub had a stock of 83 pint and half-pint glasses and there was an oilcloth on the bar floor along with seven iron and earthenware 'spittoons'. The Queen Inn was closed in 1935 when the new, State Management designed, Earl Grey opened opposite.

GOLDEN LION

Splendid exterior advertising hoardings decorate the Golden Lion in this view taken in 1898/1899 not long after the brewers Worthington's of Burton Upon Trent had paid the considerable sum of £10,000 for it, when it came up for sale in 1897. The pub is first recorded in Slater's Carlisle street directory of 1855, but there appears to be no record of it

pre this date. The property itself, however, was already built by 1842 as it is shown on Studholme's map of Carlisle but not on Wood's 1821 map. So it must have gone up at some time during the twenty years between 1822 to 1842. It should not be ruled out that it wasn't a public house pre 1855, trading under a different name.

A print of the Golden Lion circa 1892 as it looked before the alterations of 1897 which appear in the photograph and clearly show the changes. At the time of this view the wine and spirit merchants T& H Skeltons were the owners.

GOLDEN LION STORES.

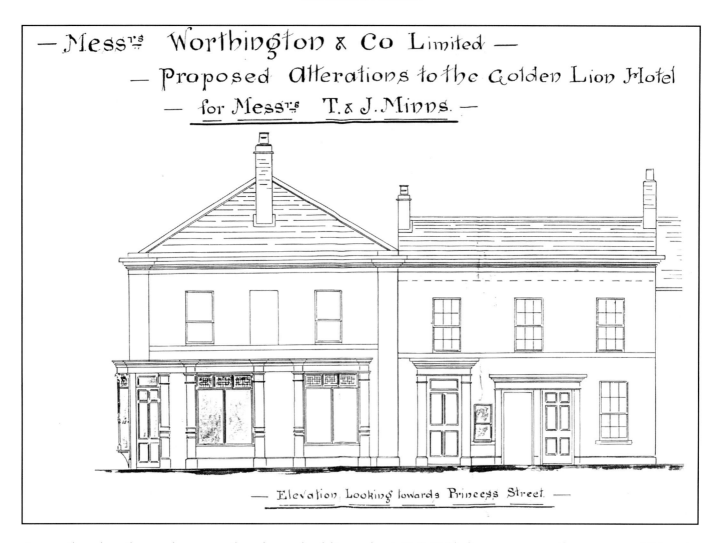

— Messrs Worthington & Co Limited —
— Proposed Alterations to the Golden Lion Hotel
— for Messrs T. & J. Minns. —

— Elevation Looking towards Princess Street. —

As mentioned on the previous page the wine and spirit merchants T & H Skeltons were one- time owners of this pub. Having acquired it in 1891 for the sum of £3,870, they eventually sold it on to Worthington's in 1897, making a very good return on their initial outlay. Worthington's decided to make alterations to the property by fitting bay windows, a new corner entrance and barrel shoots to the cellar, accessed from trap doors on the main street front in St Nicholas road. There were also interior alterations, which created an increased bar floor space and the fitting of ornamental coloured glass partitions. Some of these still survive and are most eye catching, depicting scenes in the Lake District, one of which is the Lodore Falls, however the corner door access has been done away with.

In 1897 Worthington's leased the pub to the father and son partnership of Thomas and John Minns who by this date were the most well known spirit merchants and beer bottlers in Carlisle. They operated independently of the city's breweries and carried on a bottling trade from this and other properties they leased and owned in Carlisle. They carried on right up to the state take over in 1916.

The Golden Lion's association with the bottling trade, however, was not new in 1897, as Minns was continuing a practice that had been carried on by previous owners and tenants like Skeltons and Andrew Paterson who bottled beer when he was tenant of this pub between 1880- 1891(see bottle on p 137).

ANDREW PATERSON,
GOLDEN LION HOTEL,
2 & 4 St. Nicholas Street, CARLISLE.

This Hotel having been recently enlarged and improved, Commercial Gentlemen and Private Parties will find it both comfortable and convenient.

FIVE MINUTES' WALK FROM RAILWAY STATION.

BRITISH AND FOREIGN WINES, of the best quality.

GOLDEN FLEECE

T E Nicholson took over the license to become manager of the Golden Fleece on the 4 June 1899 so this view must be after that dat but it is most certainly pre State Management because of the drink - promoting advertising on the pub's exterior. The pub was one of some 20 Carlisle properties owned/leased by the Maryport Brewery Company during the 1894 - 1916 era, but the arrival of the State scheme affected this brewery's production (output dropped by some 55%) and it triggered the brewery's demise though its eventual closure was by the State Management in November of 1921. The firms trade mark of a lion and turret can be made out and this, plus the label seen on this page, would have been multi coloured just like the brewery advertising mirror seen on page 141.

The old label shown to the left is undated and there is no reference to when the Maryport Brewery launched this brand of blended whisky but it was probably during the 1890's. Advertising cards promoting its sale can be made out in the pub window above. One point worth considering though, was how did a brewery some 30 miles from Carlisle come to have such an influence in the city's drinks trade? Well a part answer to this was the one time existence of a small brewery that was located at Dalston, owned by a W T Trimble, he had acquired a handful of Carlisle public houses during the 1880's and went on to amalgamate with the Maryport Brewery in 1891. It is not clear when the Dalston brewery closed but Mr Trimble was one of the directors of the Maryport Brewery. Co around 1900.

The Golden Fleece in the State Management years. This is a good example of how the Control Board removed the earlier colourful drink related advertising in their aim to achieve an ordinary dwelling house appearance on the city's pubs, and no doubt they were pleased with their work here in not promoting the sale of drink. The truth is though on comparing the two photographs the character of the original property has been lost and the pub in the above view has now taken on a rather uninviting and sombre appearance. This view probably dates around 1934 and the South End Constitutional Club took over in 1936.

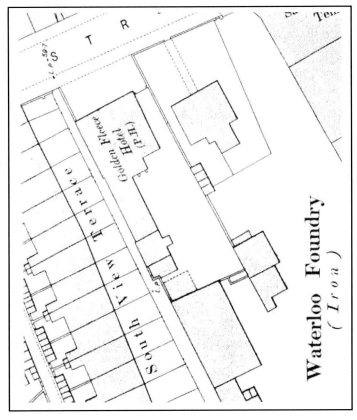

Left is the 1899 O.S map showing the Golden Fleece and the surrounding block of property including Daniel Clark's foundry. But when was the public house built? The rear of the building dates back to at least 1842, and the front was extended to St Nicholas Street in 1897. However the first record as a pub does not occur until 1858. Before this date it must have been a private dwelling house. Years later, in 1911, when T E Nicholson was in charge of what was then a much enlarged property the pub was popular in that area, as it is recorded that the Maryport Brewery delivered 216 barrels of Mild Ale, 12 barrels of I.P.B and 42 kildekins of Stout between January and June of that year. A reporter writing in the *Carlisle Journal* 12 July 1927 regretted the arrival of the State Scheme. He spoke of the 'weakness of Control products' and how 'Maryport beer was a favourite tipple, but not now obtainable.'

WHITE OX

The White Ox stood on the corner of St Nicholas Street and Woodruffe Terrace, but was closed by the State during 1919. This view of the property, now a private house, was taken during the 1980's. A mural now covers the area where the bill posting board is in this view. This mural, though well done, has no connection with the history of this building as a pub. It seems that there was a large sign fitted in this position when the building was trading as the White Ox and the photo below is a close up of part of this original exterior decoration.

The 'OX' in 2003, needing a coat of white paint.

Left: easily missed by passers by, this moulding is a rare survivor of Carlisle Victorian pub heritage. It is not exactly known what it is made from. Possibly it is cast in 'stucco' (i.e. a cement/plaster mix). It is the finishing touch to a frame made of the same material which is also still in situ. It raises the question what was the original sign inside this framework? Have the billposters, and more recently the mural, been covering over more of the original advertising, which is still intact?

WHITE OX

Turning now to the known history of the building. The property itself was built between 1849 to 1852 and it became a public house in 1872 (though it only had a beer licence). It was still a beerhouse in 1894 and it was put up for sale in the September of that year; a sales advert indicated that it had good potential for any would - be purchaser. It said that the White Ox 'was the first licensed premises on entering Carlisle from Currock and Upperby which were rapidly developing and that it already meets with a large patronage'. The Carlisle Old Brewery Co bought the pub at this sale from the original owners who were called Elsworth; the purchase price being £1,700. Despite the encouraging sale advert there is evidence that the new owners were not entirely satisfied with their acquisition, as a few years later in October 1898, the Carlisle Old Brewery were trying to gain a full licence for the White Ox. This was turned down as it was pointed out that the Golden Fleece was only 45 yards away and that several other pubs also had a spirit license in the near vicinity so: 'any increase to the already too well supplied locality is quite unnecessary'. It was at this hearing that the Old Brewery seemed to complain that the White Ox only sold 5 or 6 barrels a week and so needed a spirit licence to make the pub worthwhile retaining. Though this appeal for a 'Full' licence was turned down the White Ox did eventually get a permit to sell spirits in 1902. The pub remained the property of the Carlisle Old Brewery Co right up to the state take over in 1916.

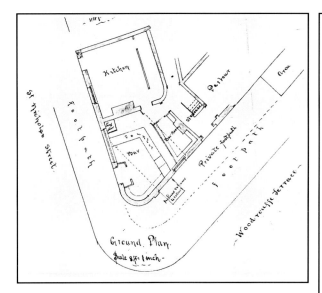

Above is a plan dating to 1879 showing the layout of the ground floor and shape and position of bar, however alterations were carried out in 1896 which could have changed this earlier arrangement. This plan was drawn up to indicate the position of a new cellar which was to be 8ft deep, with the beer shoots located off Woodruffe Terrace, though whether this awkward work was actually carried out is not known.

This photo was taken in 1957 and by then the property had been a grocer's shop. The view shows the elevation to St Nicholas Street with the original pub window and entrance still in situ at this date. This can be compared with the plan and 1980's photo on the previous page, which, as can be seen, the original window and door have been bricked up.

THE SAMSON

A view of the Samson taken between 1896 and June 1900. The reason for dating the photo to these years are that Iredale's Brewery acquired the pub at the earlier date and by June 1900 it is known that one of the city's tram line system posts had been put up in front of the pub.

 The property above dates from 1891, replacing the earlier Samson that stood on the same site. The man standing in the doorway is likely Edmund Blair who was manager of this pub from 1896 to the 4 March 1901, the pub itself being owned by Iredale's brewery at this time. The naming of the original pub and this replacement is after a steam locomotive of that name which originally ran on the old Newcastle & Carlisle Railway in 1836. It should be pointed out that the location of the pub was quite near to the site of the Newcastle & Carlisle terminus, this being located just off London Road near to where the tram depot was later built.

Below right is the 1865 Ordnance Survey map for this area and as can be seen the Samson is then part of an isolated block of property known as 'Halfway Houses'. However the 'Samson' marked on this map is the original pub of that name and is NOT the same property as that shown in the above photograph.

The history of this earlier property can be traced back to 1837 when Mary Graham had a beer house located at Halfway Houses on London Road known as the 'Steam Engine' the first record to it being called the 'Samson' does not occur until 1852. This old property eventually came up for sale in the May of 1890 and by the December a plan for the new Samson was submitted to the Carlisle planning authorities.

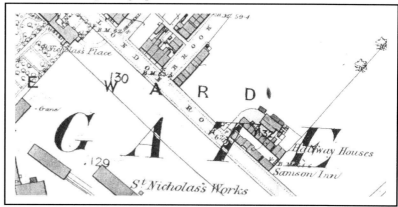

THE SAMSON

Above is the plan for the new Samson which was put before the city's Health Committee on the 19 December 1890. This new pub must have been able to accommodate more customers as the entire ground floor - area was given over to a standing bar (called a 'Vault' on the plan) some 32 feet in length and sitting customers were catered for by a 20 feet long 'snug' at the rear of the pub. However one correspondent writing to the *Carlisle Journal* 16 January 1894 mourned the loss of the old Samson and gave some interesting detail about it and some comments on its new replacement. This is what he said, 'The Samson in the 1840s or 1850s in London Road, near the old Newcastle & Carlisle station, had a signboard, which was always a pleasant picture to me. It showed the engine Samson with a train of coaches attached, Engines and coaches were of course of the style of the very early railway days and must have been painted soon after the opening of the railway. The inn was an old fashioned little house. Owned at one time by a compositor in the Journal office, my recollection of his inn is that, when you walked past it when the door was open, you always saw a bright cheery fire in the grate and a clean well kept kitchen, to give a welcome to customers, but after Joe Graham died the Samson of the old days fell before the march of improvement. In place now appears a stuccoed temple of Bacchus, with swing doors, big lamp, big counter and the other adjuncts of the modern bar. The name of the Samson is retained in stucco but the old sign of the engine is gone'.

The 1891 Samson, had however only a short existence as a public house as strangely the State Management closed it in 1917 after a life of only some 25 years. The building still stands and in recent years it has had a variety of uses one of those being a garage trading as the K Motor Co in the late 1970s early 80s.

The illustration left shows the second SAMSON steam engine which was built in 1852. There seems to be enough clues in the 1894 article to suggest that this was not the locomotive that appeared on the old signboard. However, it should be recalled that the first reference found to the pub named as the Samson occurs in 1852:

THE EARL GREY

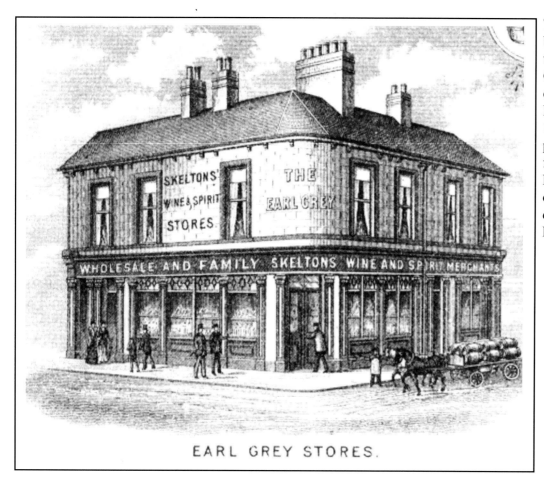

EARL GREY STORES.

This print, which dates between 1890-95 shows the late Victorian Earl Grey which stood on the corner of Union St and Botchergate from 1881/82 until it was pulled down around 1934 for the new State Management replacement of the same name. The delivery dray is in Botchergate.

This print is slightly misleading as it gives the impression that the pub stood on its own, which was not the case, as properties in both Union St and Botchergate were built up against it. Also the pub has not always occupied this position. In 1880, Arthur's Directory indicates the original Earl Grey to be the next property up from the corner (probably the building above the barrels on the dray). The corner property seen in this view was from at least 1859 to 1880, a grocers shop, but by 1882 the original Earl Grey was extended into this property. Incidentally, unlike the Golden Lion, located nearly opposite, T&H Skelton were not the owners, instead it was the Carlisle Old Brewery Co.

The first reference to the original Earl Grey is 1837, the proprietor being a James Morris who held a beer house licence. It was Mr Morris who named the pub in commemoration of Earl Grey, who between 1830-34 was prime minister and more importantly in 1832, under his leadership, the 'Reform Bill' was passed, the most important part of this legislation being that it extended the right to vote and from then on a much larger proportion of the population became eligible, no doubt including Mr Morris. *The Carlisle Journal* 17 May 1898 'Jottings' column briefly refers to this early history of the pub, it recalled 'James Morris of the Earl Grey public house Botchergate, worked at Cummersdale stampery, he was an 1832 Reformer and subsequently became a publican near the *toll bar and rechristened his house the Earl Grey' (*i.e. Botchergate/St Nicholas corner). The word rechristened is interesting as this implies there was already a pub on this site, pre -1837, trading under a different name, but this has not been tracked down.

Finally returning to the Skelton brothers association with the Earl Grey which started in 1887, the Carlisle Journal noted the death of Tom Skelton at the pub on the 28 June 1894 and went on to say he was the youngest son of the late Joe Skelton, late of Lowfield House, Wigton. Henry Skelton continued as licensee right up to the state take over in 1916. As said above, the late Victorian Earl Grey was not to survive and was replaced by a Redfearn design property in 1935.

NORTHUMBERLAND ARMS

A potential customer looks into the window of William Irving's Northumberland Arms during 1889 or 1890. The reason we know this view can be dated to these years is that the photo was taken in connection to an intended new development in Botchergate. This large block of stores and shops (known as 'Boustead's Buildings', but in later years taken up by the Co-op department stores) had building plans submitted in 1889 and by October 1891 the new block was up. The southern end of this new block extended right up to the old pub (see ink line on photo) and this obviously required the demolition of the old shops in the above view.

The wording on the gable end window reads, 'Northumberland House. Irving's Ale, Beer & Porter Stores'. The property was distinctive in that it jutted out from the building line and as a result it can be located on Wood's 1821 map. It stood not far away from the Crown Inn/Hotel site and in later years when Tait Street was built it was almost opposite. The first record of it as a pub is when a Thomas Mason had it as a beerhouse in 1840, and then in 1852 it is referred to as the 'Northumberland House',109 Botchergate.

NORTHUMBERLAND ARMS

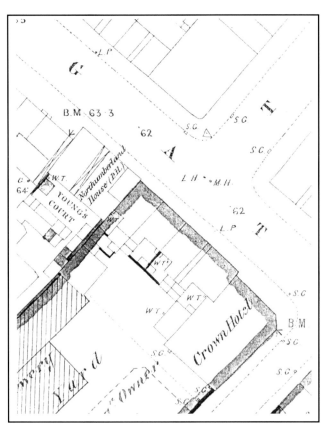

Left, the 1865 O.S map, indicating the property was then divided by a lane and as a result must have been a somewhat smaller pub during its earlier history. However, as the O S have marked the pub, this indicates it then carried a 'Full' licence, unusually though, by the early 1870's it had lost it as the premises were relegated back down to the status of a beerhouse owned or managed by a William Dillon. Then in 1877 a William Irving bought the property and he had considerable structural alterations carried out to the building in that the dividing lane was done away with so allowing the pub to be extended into what had been an adjoining shop.

Right Botchergate circa 1898, the new block of stores and shops now dominate the scene and dwarf the 'Northumberland Arms'. The pub seems to be getting the attention of a window cleaner judging by the ladders.

Mr Irving probably ran the pub as a sideline as his main trade was a wheelwright and blacksmith at 131 Botchergate where he had a forge, and by the mid 1880s he was even manufacturing kitchen ranges. Returning now to the public house. In 1894 it still just had a beerhouse licence, but as Mr Irving owned it then it was free to obtain its beer and one likely source pre 1898 must have been the nearby Crown Brewery. William Irving died in 1910 and the following is an extract from his will which was quoted in the *Carlisle Journal*, 'William Irving of 27 Tait Street, Blacksmith and Cartwright, also of the Northumberland Arms, died 20th April estate valued at £10,068, 8 shillings'.

It then looks like the Maryport Brewery bought the property, if not they certainly supplied the beer in 1911. Their sales ledger records 80 brls of Mild Ale, 6 kilders of I.P.B and 2 brls of Stout being delivered to the pub between January and June 1911. But once again the State Management was to bring to an end the history of another old Carlisle pub as they closed the Northumberland Arms on the 12 July 1916. Again, like the Samson, this action seems difficult to understand as the 'Northumberland' appeared to be a sizeable property located on a busy main street.

DEAKINS VAULTS

Presumably Edmund Bulman stands in the doorway in this view taken around 1901/02. The Carlisle New Brewery leased the pub from around 1891 and in turn they sub-let it to Mr Bulman who managed it for them but he also conducted a wine & spirit merchants business from the property. The owner of the building was a Hannah Deakin who lived in Liverpool. She had inherited the property from either her father or husband, who in turn had bought the pub around 1877 when it was called the Jovial Butcher. They started up a wine and spirit merchants trade from the pub but dropped the Jolly Butcher name changing it to Deakin's Vaults. The history of the property as the Jovial Butcher can be traced back to 1828 when it is referred to in *Pigot's Directory*. At some date after 1902 Hannah Deakin sold the pub to the Maryport Brewery as they were recorded as the owners in 1916 when the State Management took over the pub, however by the year's end they had closed it. Surprisingly what had been the old pub was still standing as late as 1966, though it was demolished in the autumn of that year.

Left is the 1899 O.S map, showing the location of the pub to have been next door to the Albion (now the Border Rambler), note the Albion did not front Botchergate like it does these days. Instead there were two shops which reduced the pub in size, the main entrance being off Portland Place, though the Albion could be accessed from Botchergate by a narrow passage between the two shops. These shops were done away with in 1905 so bringing about the size of the modern day Border Rambler.

ISMAYS VAULTS

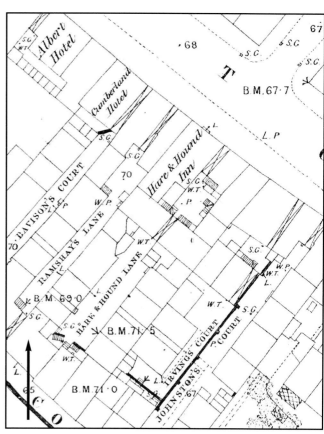

Above, the 1865 O.S. map, the arrow indicates the property that was/became the pub.

Left, Collier Lane in 2001 and the somewhat ruinous property arrowed is what remains of Ismay's Vaults

Of all the licensed properties that were in late Victorian Carlisle few, if any, readers will have heard of this one. No maps mark it, no licensed registers list it and there seems to be just one entry for it in a Carlisle street directory. The main evidence for its existence is a set of architects' plans which survive in Carlisle Records Office and are reproduced on the following page. The pub could be accessed straight off Collier Lane or down a short flight of steps from Hare and Hound Lane, which had an outlet to Botchergate (see map above). The Collier Lane pub was the property of the owner of the Hare and Hound and during the late 1880's this happened to be a George Ismay and it remained in his family's possession until the State takeover.

The word 'Vault' implies a cellar or store, but in Northern England (it seems to have its origins in Lancashire) the word was also in use to describe a simply furnished bar room. In fact these types of pubs or rooms usually offered only standing accommodation for drinkers and in the main their customers were working class men. Here, in respect to this particular property, this alternative meaning for the word 'Vault', (judging by the plans) seems to be the likely explanation for the pub's name.

Because of the lack of records it is impossible to say anything much about the pubs history, Woods1821 map of Carlisle indicates that there were buildings occupying this area of Collier Lane at that time and it could be that the property in the above photo dates back to that period, though when it became a licensed house is not known. The Ordnance Survey do not indicate the pub on their 1899 map. However, the pub must have been open at the time the map was surveyed as it is mentioned in a scrutiny of some of Carlisle's pubs carried-out by the local temperance party in September 1899. It briefly refers to the Collier Lane pub with its three - door access and, interestingly, it says 'a nice place to catch railway men'.

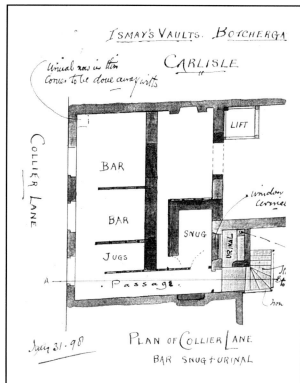

Above: the front of the pub as it would have looked from 1898. This elevation is from standing in Collier lane. The pub had a most unusual exterior in that it did not possess the usual large display window and oddly it was accessed via three stall-like doors. This elevation was drawn up for the addition of the over lights above the doors. Despite these alterations the interior (even though it would have been gas lit) must still have been rather gloomy.

Above: plan view of the ground floor as it would have been laid out from 1898. Note the rather crude corner urinal, sited in the bar itself. This interior plan shows it was going to be done away with. An improved 'snug' was also being fitted at the time. The compartment marked 'jugs' was an area given over to customers who wanted a carry-out for home consumption.

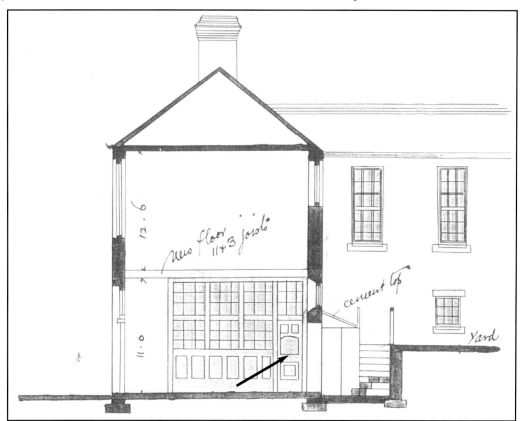

Above: section through the building on line A-B (see plan above). This view shows the step down in level from Hare and Hound yard to enable access to the pub from that direction. The door arrowed gave access to the 'snug'.

RAILWAY TAVERN

Above: This photo was taken to show the store of J G Parker, ironmonger and hardware dealer. However the camera angle also gives us the two older adjacent properties and at, what was then, 37a Botchergate, stood the original Railway Tavern. The reason for the photo, was because this block of property was soon to be pulled-down for a new development (though as it turned out Parker's store was retained). *The Carlisle Journal* 8 December 1896 reported, 'New hotel Botchergate for Mr Rickerby. Where the Railway Tavern now is. They are going to pull down this rickerty old public house and the cottages behind and erect a new hotel on the site.' This new development had been completed by the 7 September 1897 when the *Carlisle Journal* again reported, 'Railway Tavern Botchergate, has been replaced by a new house a great improvement to the city'.

Right: the 1865 O S map showing the old Railway Tavern and this can be compared to the photo above. The property was part of the block that stood between the Caledonian and Portland Place. Note in the above photo how the house is split at street level with the pub occupying the right- hand side of the property and what appears to be a shop to its left. The earliest reference for the Railway Tavern is 1861 but the history of a pub on this site goes a little further back than that. In 1834 at what was then 19 Botchergate stood a pub called the Saddle and virtually next door to it at 21 was another pub called the Indian King. As there are no maps that mark the location of Carlisle's early 19th century pubs and the fact

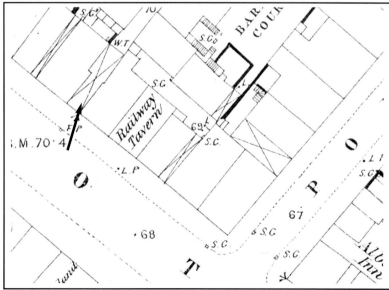

that street numbering in Botchergate changed during that century, it would have proved very difficult to pin point the exact location as to where in Botchergate these pubs had stood. Fortunately, the above 1865 O S map provides part of the answer as it marks the position of a Saddle Lane (this is arrowed on the above map). Almost certainly this means the Saddle pub had been one of the properties immediately left or right of the arrow. The Saddle was closed by 1844, but the pub at 21 Botchergate that had been the Indian King

RAILWAY TAVERN

Left: the new development is now up so this photo must have been taken after September 1897. The new 'Railway Tavern' and the entrance to Rickerbys agricultural implement stores stand on the exact spot where the old pub had been. The access to what had been Saddle Lane was retained and this now led to the Agricultural Hall. This new development extended to the right just outside this view, taking out where the old cloggers shop had been, but not Parkers stores. The new Railway Tavern was never tied to a brewery, instead it remained the property of J.Rickerby, though the Carlisle New Brewery had a spell of supplying their beer from 1901. The pub was closed by the State Management about 1917 and all this property seen here was demolished about 1998/99.

had by 1844 undergone a name change to the Andrew Marvel. By 1855 the name was changed again to the Golden Quoit and then finally, by 1861, it was called the Railway Tavern. Confirmation that the Golden Quoit was the same pub as the Railway Tavern was given by a pensioner writing to the *Cumberland News* in 1972 with information that he must have been given when a youngster, that the Railway Tavern had formerly been called the Golden Quoit and that there had been a Ropery (i.e a rope works) located at the back of the pub. It seems then, that the old Railway Tavern property seen in the photo on the previous page had carried four names between 1834 and its demolition in 1897.

A comment now on the name Andrew Marvel. This is an unusual title for a public house, his name suggests that he may have been a 19th century music hall or circus strongman of local or national fame, who perhaps performed amazing feats of strength, these type of performers were not uncommon in Victorian Britain. In reality though the answer turns out to be much different. He was born way back in 1621 and was a poet and M.P. for Hull for most of his life, until he died in 1678. Hull, the city Marvel went to school in, did not forget him, as there was a public house named after him and a statue to him was put up in the 1860's. Though why his name came to be used for a public house in Carlisle remains a mystery.

ALBERT HOTEL

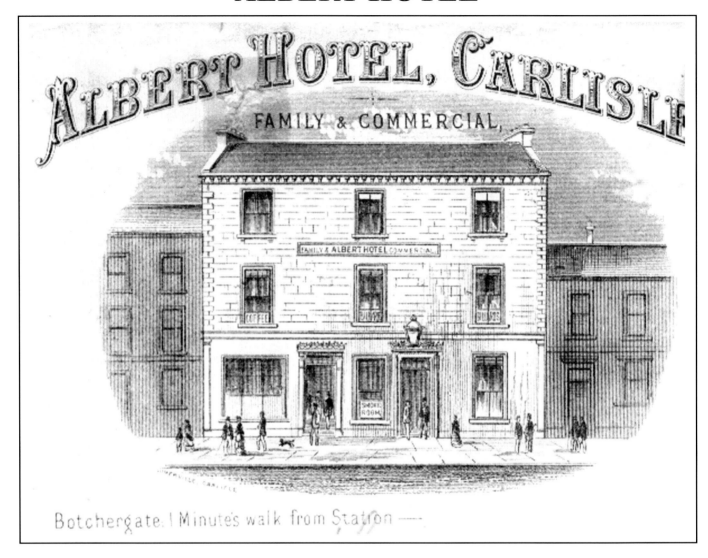

This engraving is taken from a billhead and shows the Albert as it would have looked from circa 1880 up to closure in 1892. The print has been somewhat exaggerated in that the property depicted stands out from the building line and the surrounding structures are made to look faint, small, and lacking in detail. In fact immediately to the Albert's left stood the original Victorian Cumberland Hotel. This building was higher in elevation and also it would have been a competitor for trade, so it is not surprising that the artist has omitted it from the above advertisement.

The Albert is first listed in a Carlisle street directory for 1855 and almost certainly was named after Queen Victoria's husband. By the 1870's the property was owned by Iredale's brewery and during the 1880's it was well known for its billiard tables. However, it seems that billiards was not the only attraction to customers. On the 12 July 1892 the *Carlisle Journal* reported: 'The Albert hotel is the habitual resort of women of bad character and there is drunkenness on the premises.' The Carlisle licensing register book which lists the pub from 1887-1892 reveals that these women were in fact prostitutes. During these years a few other Carlisle public houses were associated with women of 'bad character,' but in the case of the Albert it seems that this was not going to be tolerated and was the main cause of bringing about the pubs closure when the licence came-up to be renewed in September 1892. After closure it became the Botchergate Conservative Club opening on the 28 August 1893. However, nuisances were still to be associated with the property as only two months later men were being asked to leave who were not members, and there was a letter to the paper complaining about the club and drunkenness. It's management can not have improved much over the years as on the 14 July 1903 the *Carlisle Journal* reported that the 'Botchergate Conservative Club had been struck off the register, there being continual drunkenness on the premises, though there was nothing to stop its continuance as a club, but not with a drink licence'. It is not clear whether this action by the licensing magistrates caused the immediate closure of the club but, by 1912 it was no longer based at the property and the ground floor was occupied by a newsagents and shoe shop.

CALEDONIAN

The dissolution of the partnership of the Carlisle wine and spirit merchants Nicholson & Skelton on the 20.1.1905 caused 3 Carlisle public houses to come onto the property market at the same time. Unusually for the period a pictorial sales catalogue was produced and the above photo of the 'Caley' is taken from this brochure.

The Caledonian was one of the most popular city pubs between the years 1894-1916 and did a large trade. The naming of the property is linked to the Scottish railway company of that name which arrived in the city during 1847. The first reference to it is in 1852 when it was called the Lancaster& Caledonian Hotel at 12 Botchergate Then on the 15.12.1854 the *Carlisle Journal* reported, 'John Birney has rebuilt the Caledonian Hotel at very great expense'. It is likely from this information that we can say that the building in the above photo dates to 1854. However the C.J for the 26.5.1863 reported a fire at the Caledonian, though it is not known how much damage was caused to the building because of it.

After 1905 it seems the Maryport brewery undertook to supply the beer. Some idea of the amount of trade this pub did can be had from one of the brewery's surviving sales ledgers dating to 1911. Apart from supplying their own draught and bottled beers they also continued to supply the big name brands. In the month of January 1911 the Maryport brewery supplied 46 barrels of their own beer,4 Hogsheads (1 hogshead = 54 gallon) of Bass No 6 Ale, 3 Hogs of Bass Pale Ale, 1 barrel of Worthington's, 2 Kilderkins of Guinness, 4 Firkins of Bass No 1 Ale, 1 Pin of Irish Whisky, 6 Pins of Old Blended Glenlivet (1 Pin = 4 and a half gallons) and 12 crates of bottled Stout.

It is interesting to note that the pub was linked to the railway in more than just its name as John Minns indicated in his 1934 article that railwaymen were predominantly its customers and this practice probably continued into the State Management years.

OLD CITY AREA

The title above is best described as that area once bounded by the city walls. This area ,which is roughly triangular, could be said to be bounded by the Castle, West and East Tower Street, along Lowther Street to the Citadel/Court towers and back towards the castle via West Walls. A few of the public houses in the list below were not strictly inside this boundary, but near enough to group them into this area. The licensed properties located within the city confines were generally the oldest and the 'Kings Head' and the 'Sportsman' are Carlisle's earliest surviving pubs that are still open for trade. This area also contained the largest concentration of public houses in Carlisle in 1894, with some 34 named licensed properties. Keeping this in mind it is remarkable that today's beer enthusiast will only be able to find four of these pubs still open. The main reasons for this were the closures carried out by the State Scheme from 1916 onwards and the earlier temperance-inspired purge . Many of the pubs in this area were located in lanes and this may be the reason why so few were recorded photographically.

Some of the regulars of the Kings Head stand in Rosemary Lane. This view can be dated between 1903-1909 when J.Lawson held the managers licence for this pub. The photo indicates that the pub was then accessed from the lane and

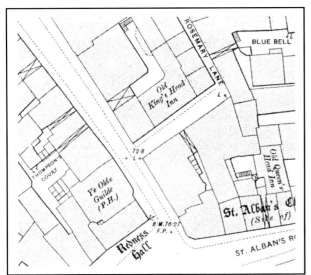

this is confirmed by the 1899 O S map, there being no frontage to Fisher Street at this time. Above the queue at the end of the lane and standing in Fisher Street was the City Vaults and this can just be made out in the above view. This was owned by Graham's Caldewgate brewery and it was nicknamed the 'Klondike.' Confusingly the Ordnance survey have marked the pub as the 'Ye Olde Guilde,' a short-lived name and a possible error.

OLD CITY AREA

The following is a list of all 34 named licensed properties located in this area at 1894. Once again those printed in bold are covered in more detail in the following pages.

1. **GAOL TAP** — DEMOLISHED 1930
2. **WELLINGTON** — NOW SITE OF YATES WINE LODGE
3. FRIARS — STILL OPEN
4. **ROSE AND CROWN** — CLOSED 1911 BUT PROPERTY STILL STANDING
5. DOG AND BULL — LOCATED IN PEASCODS LANE CLOSED 1903/04
6. **CROWN AND ANCHOR** — CLOSED 1927
7. OLD BUSH — OLD BUSH LANE/ CLOSED CIRCA 1918
8. LION AND LAMB — DISLICENSED/ RENAMED THE TRADES HALL 1917
9. GLOBE INN — CLOSURE DATE NOT KNOWN
10. THREE CANNONS — THREE CANNONS LANE CLOSED 12.7.1916
11. BLUE BELL — CLOSED 1973
12. HOLE IN THE WALL — CLOSED 1921
13. **KINGS HEAD** — STILL OPEN
14. CITY VAULTS — CLOSED 1921
15. **ORDNANCE ARMS** — CLOSED 1903
16. **BLACK BULL VAULTS** — BECAME IRISH GATE TAVERN IN 1917
17. SARACENS HEAD — BECAME IRISH GATE TAVERN 1917
18. WRESTLERS ARMS — ANNETWELL STREET/CLOSED 1911
19. **BIRD IN HAND** — CLOSED 12.7.1916
20. **SPREAD EAGLE** — CLOSED 27.2.1903
21. LIVERPOOL ARMS — CLOSED 11.10.1916
22. QUARTER OF MUTTON — CLOSED 1898
23. QUEENS HEAD HOTEL — CLOSED 1903
24. ANGEL — CLOSED 1916 * also had a spell when it was called Bewsher's Vaults
25. **SHAKESPEARE** — CLOSED BETWEEN 1920-30
26. **FISH AND DOLPHIN** — CLOSED 1913
27. **FARMERS ARMS** — CLOSED 1906
28. **LOWTHER ARMS** — CLOSED 1914/15
29. **SPORTSMAN** — STILL OPEN
30. COACH AND HORSES — BLACKFRIARS STREET/CLOSED 12.7.1916
31. FISH INN — CLOSED 1907
32. WHITE HORSE VAULTS — INCORPORATED INTO THE BUSH HOTEL
33. APPLE TREE — REBUILT BY REDFERN 1927
34. **HOWARD ARMS** — STILL OPEN

The following pubs were in the very near vicinity so they are grouped into this area.

1. CALEDONIAN (ENGLISH DAMSIDE) — CLOSED 19.10.1916
2. NEW INN (MOUNSEYS COURT) this was located off English Damside — CLOSED 27.2.1903
3. CROWN — CLOSED 12.7.1916
4. **LORD BROUGHAM** — CLOSED 1932

GAOL TAP

Above, the City Arms but popularly referred to by most Carlisle folk of the time by the nick name of the 'Gaol Tap' is seen here sometime between 1897 and June 1900. The former date was when the brewers Worthington's began supplying the beer and the latter date was the start of the Carlisle electric tram system, by June 1900 one of the posts carrying the overhead wires had been fixed into position in front of the building and this can be seen in the photo on the next page.

   The distinctive curved entrance to the pub with its pediment depicting the City Arms, dated from 1858 and was built onto the end of existing property. This extension can clearly be made out when comparing the two maps below. The map on the left dates to 1853, numbers 41 and 42 English Street would, five years later, be part of the newly arrived City Vaults/Gaol Tap but at 1853 they were a grocer's and wine and spirit merchants shops, number 43 being a pub called the Pine Apple. The map on the right dates to 1865.

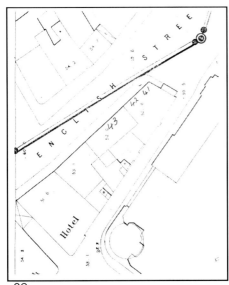

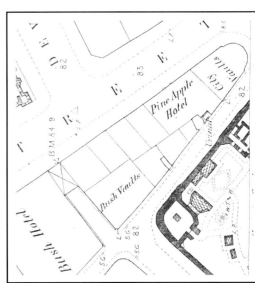

Above: this view of the pub would date between June 1900 to the summer of 1916. It is almost certain that the photo would be no later than July/August 1916, as by this date the State Management had started removing drink- promoting advertisements from the city's pubs. Note the name 'Pinearies' displayed on the pub exterior in the above photo, this was a reference to the Pine Apple which at one time had taken up that part of the building and the area marked by the arrow. This was a separate public house, being divided off from the City Vaults (see 1865 map on previous page). The Pine Apple was the original public house located in this block of property and can be traced back to at least 1847, but by 1875 it had closed and was in use as a grocer's shop. Then about ten years later the wine and spirit merchants, Halstead and Pearson, who owned the adjacent City Arms/Gaol Tap, bought the property that had been the Pine Apple and extended their pub through into that building. John Reay the Carlisle wine and spirit merchant acquired the newly enlarged pub circa 1888 and in 1897 leased it to John Minns, who was to manage right up until the State takeover (this regime did not close it and it remained open up to 28 October 1930).

There is little doubt that the 'Gaol Tap' was Carlisle's most impressive late Victorian pub and there are quite a few surviving photos of it, yet surprisingly there are none known showing its interior. It is recorded, however, that the interior like its exterior was of smart appearance and that there were two big smoke rooms upstairs 'beautifully appointed' and with massive marble fireplaces. In the early Carlisle United years, the pub was very popular when a home fixture was on, the pub being 'packed to capacity' before a match and apparently at these times the pub would have a whole brewing in the cellar to meet demand.

Some years earlier, though (17 May 1898), the cellar was the scene of a tragedy when a Charles Forester, who was employed as a barman, fell down the steps and was killed. Continuing with unpleasant occurrences associated with the 'Gaol Tap' the *Carlisle Patriot* newspaper reported on 15 September 1899 a 'Mad Act'. Apparently a customer of the pub who had gone in for a drink between eight and nine o'clock in the morning (Victorian public houses were then open from 6 a m to 11 p m) and who was already intoxicated at the time, was refused drink. Being ordered out he went away quietly. However he returned with a granite road 'set' and put it right through the large ornamented bent sheet of plate glass. Luckily, it seems there were no casualties to the customers inside the pub. Trouble at the city's public houses is nothing new and it is known that the 'Gaol Tap' even had a bouncer employed at this time who was referred to as the 'chucker out'. The pub was bought by the Corporation in 1928 so that it could be demolished, along with the gaol, for street widening and new shops. The pub was levelled by the end of 1930 and Woolworths was built on part of the site in 1932.

WELLINGTON

The Wellington stood virtually opposite the 'Gaol Tap' and this was another pub that was associated with the Carlisle wine and spirit firm of T & J Minns but unlike the 'Gaol Tap' this pub was their own property having acquired it in April 1905 from the owners and spirit merchants Nicholson and Skelton. Note the advert in the window referring to the 'Baronial Hall'. This was fitted into the pub during 1906 and dismantled by the State Management in 1916, so the above photo must have been taken at some time between these dates. The Wellington was described in the sale brochure of January 1905 as of 'modern construction.' The date when this occurred seems to be 1854. It replaced an earlier pub that had stood on the site which was also called the Wellington for a short spell, but this building had traded for a longer time under its earlier name of the French Horn. The property is known to have been a 'small thatched house' and had stood here from at least 1828.

Left, the Worthingtons bottle car stands outside the pub sometime after 1905. It was on a visit to the city to promote the brewery's beers and stopped outside those Carlisle licensed houses that the brewery supplied or owned. This car must have been quite a good advertising attraction in its day and would have toured around Britain's towns and cities. Visits to those at a distance from Burton Upon Trent may have required the vehicle to have been carried by rail. A similar but later bottle car survives and can be seen at the Bass museum at Burton

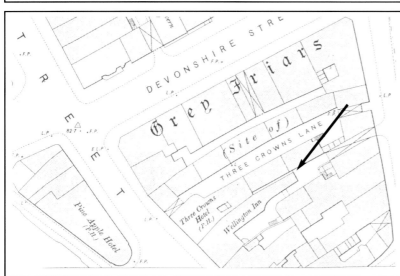

Left, the 1899 O.S map. The arrow indicates the position of where in the property the 'Baronial Hall' was located. In 1904 Three Crowns Lane became the site of the 'Arcade'and these days Yates wine lodge can be accessed from it. The site of the Wellington is also occupied by Yates. Note the Ordnance Survey have marked the City Vaults/Gaol Tap as the 'Pine Apple'.

Above, two views of the 'Baronial Hall' taken from a souvenir booklet titled *Ye Old Baronial Hall* produced by John Minns in 1918, shortly after it had been gutted by the Central Liquor Traffic Control Board (i.e. the State Management). The room was fitted out with oak panelling and doors, suits of armour ,helmets, shields and pole-axes. Minns souvenir booklet says, 'it gave such a feeling of peace and contentment as if you had stepped back into the days of old when knights were bold.' There is little doubt that the 'Baronial Hall' was years ahead of its time and these days it would have been classed as a 'theme pub.' If any reader wants further information about this odd Edwardian public house attraction, then a copy of the souvenir booklet mentioned above is in Carlisle Library.

ROSE AND CROWN

A view of the Rose and Crown taken in 1978. The property still stands today and is located in Lowthians Lane. The original pub window (next to the modern lamp post) has a bar fitted across. This insignificant item was actually quite important as it is thought it allowed outside drinking in the lane to take place. As long as the drinker had one hand on the rail then he was not breaking the law. It is not known how many other brass bars were fitted to other Carlisle pubs and it may have been unique. Whatever, there must have been a virtual scrum to get hold of the bar or to get back inside the pub when the 'bobbies' came down the lane. Though, being 'cannie' drinkers, they probably had look-outs positioned for such an unwanted disturbance anyway.

The first record for a Rose and Crown in Lowthians lane occurs in 1829 but, being in the city centre, it is likely that the history of the pub goes back into the 18th century.

It is known that a Mr T G R Nanson bought the property in 1866. He was a wine and spirit merchant and in later years owned a public house located in West Tower Street and marked on the 1899 O.S map as 'Nansons Vaults'. No further events or history is known about the Rose and Crown during the later Victorian years. Its demise though was not due to the arrival of the State Management but instead began in 1908. *The Carlisle Journal* reported 4 February 1908 that at the annual Carlisle licensing sessions, the magistrates had refused to renew the pub's licence. The reasons given were that the premises were 'badly ventilated, badly lighted, insanitary, structurally unfit, unnecessary for the requirements of the district and not capable of proper supervision.'

The magistrates would compensate the owners for the intended closure and appointed a valuer; this was carried out in early June 1908. It was said the pub was in a narrow lane and would only be of use as a warehouse, his valuation being just £200. There must have been some dispute over the low valuation and the pub got a temporary renewal of its license as it continued to trade through 1908 and 1909. In July 1910 the authorities improved their compensation offer to £900 but this was refused by the owners of the Rose and Crown and the pub remained open into 1911. But in the June of that year the dispute over an acceptable compensation for the closure and financial loss to the owners was resolved and acceptable terms must have been agreed as the *Carlisle Journal* 9 June 1911 reported, 'executors of T G R Nanson to sell contents, premises to be closed under compensation award.' The Rose and Crown does not appear in the list of public houses in the 1912/13 Carlisle street directory.

CROWN AND ANCHOR

This pub was located just off Scotch Street in the lane that was eventually named after it. The earliest reference found so far, occurs in the *Carlisle Journal* for 1814, where it is briefly referred to in no more than a one-line entry as being for sale. In 1828 it is listed in the first Carlisle street directory, which name the city's licensed properties. Pigot's 1828/29 directory lists the Crown and Anchor as then being located in Old Turks Head Lane, owned or tenanted by a John Elliot. This seems to indicate that the lane had at one time a pub in it called the Old Turks Head. Possibly at some date pre-1814 this pub had undergone a name change to the Crown and Anchor. However to confuse the situation further the Carlisle street directory for 1829, (Parson & White) lists the Crown and Anchor still run by John Elliot but now the lane is referred to as Jollie's lane. The directory for 1834 lists the Crown and Anchor as in Crown and Anchor lane and obviously the lane has finally been renamed. There are of course many public houses throughout Britain known by the name of the Crown and Anchor; the meaning of this title is apparently linked to ex - seamen who were in the Royal Navy (the crown and anchor being an arm badge of the R N). Having done their service some returned to town life and bought or became a tenant of a public house and on taking over the property, if the opportunity allowed, renamed it to this sign. By the 1890s the Carlisle Old Brewery were the owners and the Carlisle Journal for 13 April 1897 reported plans for alterations to the Crown and Anchor. These were stated to be 'rebuilding of an old dilapidated building and enlarging the bedroom accommodation.' The word rebuilding is surely misleading as a glance at the photo indicates that the exterior is certainly pre-1897. This exterior work planned in 1897 to the so-called 'dilapidated' building was more likely a reference to an intended re-roofing job also the ground floor windows were likely enlarged at this time. Turning now to the final years of the Crown and Anchor. The pub cleared the hurdle of the early closures by the State Management which took place between 1916 -1919, but was closed in 1927, being delicensed it was sold off to a Mr Routledge for a sum of £1,000 in September of that year. The photo above was taken before demolition in 1979.

ORDNANCE ARMS

This view, also comes from the Minns collection of Carlisle public houses, as said elsewhere in this publication most of these old photos date to 1901/02. However there are five which seem to have been taken slightly earlier and this pub is one of them as Chris Little was the licensee from 1894-July 1897. The first reference to the property as the Ordnance Arms occurs in the 1828/29 street directories. However note the adjacent lane next to the pub was called the Three Cannons. This sounds like a pub name (there was one at the foot of Scotch street) and it shouldn't be ruled out that the Ordnance at some time pre 1828 carried this name. The meaning of the Ordnance Arms name is certainly linked to the nearby castle, ordnance being artillery or military stores.

The demise of the pub was caused by the corporation who wanted to carry out street improvements to this area which would require the demolition of existing old property including the pub. These plans brought about its closure which took place on the 27 February 1903. However the threat of demolition to the Ordnance Arms had begun in 1899, but at this time it was not the city council who wanted to pull it down, but the owners themselves; the Carlisle Old Brewery Co. The plan was for a brand new larger pub (presumably still to be called the Ordnance Arms). In order to build this the Old Brewery proposed to demolish the block of property, including the pub, up to Castle lane (see map). The brewery made a case to the Carlisle licensing magistrates that this proposal would be a benefactory improvement to that area as the existing property was described as old and insanitary. But there were objections from the military authorities in charge of the garrison at the castle and also from an adjacent salvation army building. It was said by the opponents that the proposal was to 'erect a huge gin palace at the castle gates' and that it was a barefaced attempt to add largely to the drinking facilities of the city. The commander at the castle said, 'he had the strongest possible objections to the plan.' It was said the house could be put 'out of bounds' but that would need additional supervision by the military police and it would be a temptation to men to disobey orders. This opposition effectively killed the plan and the scheme never went ahead. Today the site of the Ordnance Arms lies beneath Castle Way.

BLACK BULL VAULTS

The earliest reference to the Old Black Bull is 1829. But this date is not for the property in the above photo but relates to an earlier Black Bull that stood on the same site. The property shown above dates to 1878/79, being put up by Charles Dudson, a Carlisle builder. In fact at the time the view above was taken (late 1904/early 1905) the property had only been standing for some 26 years. The licensing register for 1894 and some of the Carlisle street directories still list it as the Old Black Bull, i.e. continuing the name of the one-time original pub it replaced. A variation on the name was the Black Bull Vaults and this is carried on the window advertising in the photograph. However the name that made this Carlisle pub famous was the nickname of the 'Blazing Barrel' and as such it became somewhat immortalised to future generations of Carlisle drinkers.

The barrel was in fact made of red glass and was gas-lit from the inside so turning it into a lamp and this obviously explains the origins of the pub's nickname. The barrel had been on the building from circa 1879 being the idea of Mr Dudson the owner and builder of the property, but he had some difficulties in getting permission for it to be fitted there as there were strong objections from the local temperance movement. It is not known what happened to the barrel, but presumably it was removed by the State Management in their purge against drink-promoting advertising.

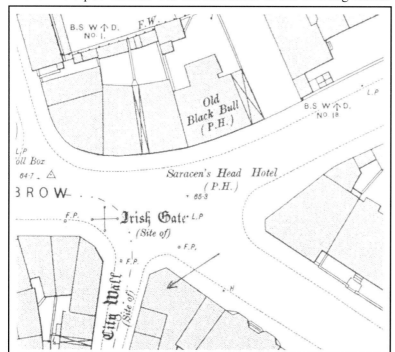

Left: is the 1899 O.S map. The arrow marks the site of Chivers sports shop and this should enable the reader to get his bearings. Note the Saracens Head was next door to the Black Bull. This pub had also been rebuilt replacing a much earlier property of that name that had stood on the site.

A good view of the pub in 1902 , note the star fitted above the barrel this was also gas-lit but it seems it was a short-lived decoration as it is thought that it was only fitted during the celebrations for King Edward VII's Coronation. The Black Bull had a long association with the Carlisle wine and spirit merchants Nicholson and Skelton who were the proprietors from 1880 - 1905, the latter year being when they put the pub up for sale. The following information about the pub is extracted from the 1905 sales brochure. It was said to be 'one of the best known and most popular in the city and was in touch with a large working men's locality. It has a frontage of 47ft and a depth of 69ft; the bar is 29 feet long. The cellar accommodation is one of the features of the premises, being lofty and well-ventilated and providing gantry room for 29 Hogsheads.'

BLACK BULL VAULTS

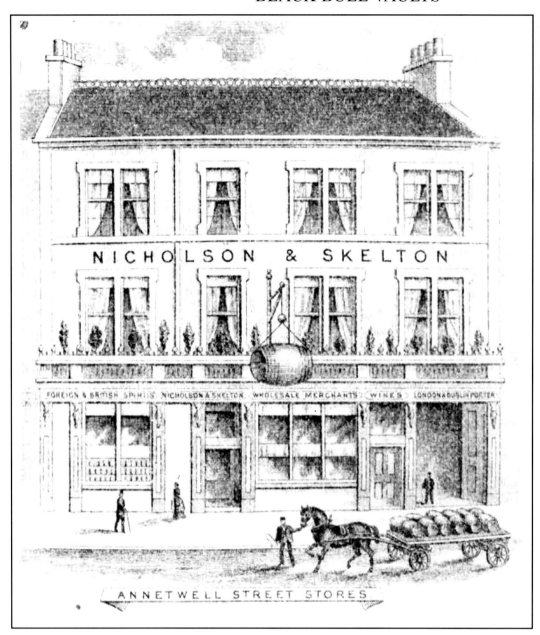

ANNETWELL STREET STORES

Left: an early view of the Black Bull taken from a printed billhead dating circa 1881. Note there is no gas-lit star fitted at this date.

The man who replaced Nicholson and Skelton as owner, Joseph Bouch, would have been well known to them as he had been their manager in the Wellington for the previous 20 years. He purchased the Black Bull in the spring of 1905 for £7,250, but it was an unusual transaction, as Bouch had very little cash to his name. Skelton actually loaned him part of the purchase money this being £5,000 and he raised the rest from the Maryport Brewery Co. This speculative move by Mr Bouch turned out to be a bad one as two years later he was in the bankruptcy courts. It is difficult to be certain from the surviving records what had gone wrong to cause this. Bouch himself said 'there was no trade at that end of town, they could see any amount of men propping up the bridges.' A possible explanation for these comments is a suggestion that there were too many other public houses in the near vicinity and 'propping up the bridges' could mean there was a temporary slump causing men to be out of work and obviously this would affect trade. It has to be kept in mind though that these were Bouch's own explanations, as there seems to be some evidence the failure of the business lay with him. Just three years later the new owners of the Black Bull, the Maryport Brewery Co were selling 9 barrels of beer a week. Whatever caused Bouch's unfortunate circumstances between 1905-1907, he unintentionally left his mark in the history of Carlisle's public houses by using glass bottles which carry his and the pub's name. These have been occasionally found buried in old Carlisle ash tips. They are rare and as a result are quite sought after by local bottle collectors.

As said above the Maryport Brewery became the owners after Bouch and they remained so until the arrival of the State scheme in 1916. The State now in charge of the city's pubs had plans for the Black Bull namely to convert it into the Irish Gate Tavern. This involved knocking through into the adjoining Saracens Head, so enlarging the property. This alteration was completed by the October of 1917. As the Irish Gate Tavern it stood until 1972, when it was demolished for Castle Way, part of the Inner Ring Road scheme.

BIRD IN HAND

A view of the Bird in Hand about 1902. The Carlisle New Brewery had held this pub on a short lease in 1900 but in November 1901 Iredale's started supplying the beer under a 5 year lease. The pub itself was privately owned by a Mr Riddell of Brampton. The man standing in the doorway is presumably George Lewthwaite he had been a hatter by trade, living in Denton Holme before he took over the license in 1895. The pub stood in Castle Street virtually opposite the entrance to Tullie House. It was closed by the state on the 12 July1916.

The earliest reference for the Bird in Hand occurs in both the 1828/29 Carlisle street directories, when a John Dunn was licensee. His name crops up again in a licensing document that dates to 1813 for a public house in Castle Street. Unfortunately this document fails to name the pub, but it is likely that this is an earlier indication to the presence of the Bird in Hand. However, the situation is not straightforward as there were other pubs located in Castle Street pre 1829 and possibly his name was linked to one of these before the Bird in Hand was established. These were the Ship (referred to in 1803 gone by 1829), the Punch Bowl (referred to in 1803 gone by 1829), the Woodman (referred to in 1806 gone by 1829) and the Masons Arms (referred to in 1814 gone by 1829). Another line of thought is that any one of the previously mentioned pubs could have been renamed to the Bird in Hand.

The meaning of the name Bird in Hand is interesting. Apparently it became popular as a British pub sign during the 18th century but there are a number of origins to how the name came about. The most interesting is that it was adapted from the old proverb, to become 'One drink in the bird in hand is worth two in the bush,' the Bush being any nearby rival pub.

SPREAD EAGLE

Described in 1899 as 'one of the oldest licensed houses in the city', the history of the Spread Eagle can be traced back to at least 1795 when it gets a brief mention in the *Cumberland Pacquet* newspaper of that year. The licensee or owner at this time being a Jacob Johnston.

The view left was taken about 1902 and again shows the sur-name Johnston linked to this pub (he was a tenant). However, in the intervening years between 1795 and 1895 there were many other family names associated with the Spread Eagle.

The inn was reached (indicated by the arrow on the plan) up a narrow lane which carried the same name as the pub and as can be seen opened out into a yard. The pub looks small judging by the frontage, but a glance at the O S map shows this view to be misleading. The following details about the Spread Eagle date to 1899.

'The house is in a good situation, adjacent to the potato market, and does an excellent business being one of the oldest licensed houses in the city. It provides a cool and spacious beer cellar for 18 barrels, wine and spirit cellars, 2 snugs, smoking room, bar, kitchen, market room, large sitting room and 8 good bedrooms. The front and back yards are spacious and the requirements of the large number of country and city customers are fully met'. The rear of the Spread Eagle was accessed from St Cuthbert's lane where beer shoots to the cellar were located and also a range of stables to accommodate farmers' horses on market days. Unfortunately, the Spread Eagle was to be an early closure, this event taking place on the 27 February 1903. The property was pulled down for the new Crown and Mitre Hotel development.

See a token from this pub on page 130.

ST CUTHBERT'S LANE

The 1899 Ordnance Survey map showing the three fully licensed public houses at that time, which were, 1. Fish and Dolphin, 2. Lowther Arms, 3. Shakespeare Tavern, the Farmers Arms was a beerhouse and because of that the Ordnance survey omitted to mark the location of these type of licensed houses in the city. So I have marked its site with the arrow.

A view of the Farmers' Arms when Robert Bell was the licensee, which means this photo must have been taken pre-June 1901 as R. Lockerbie took over as manager after that date. The Carlisle street directories indicate that Mr Bell had a long run at the Farmers Arms being its licensee from at least 1869. This view of the property is in the direction of looking up the lane towards St Cuthbert's church.

FISH AND DOLPHIN

These views of the Fish and Dolphin and those on the following page are taken from a set of six or seven photographs (the whereabouts of the originals is now unknown). They were taken when Robert Pearson was the licensee, which means they are no earlier than 1911 and not later than 1913 as the pub was closed during that year. In fact it seems very likely that they were taken in 1913 being produced as evidence to the licensing magistrates in an attempt to keep the pub open.

The above view is looking at the pub in the direction of St Cuthbert's church, the door nearest the camera led to the public bar. The photo opposite is looking down the lane in the other direction and part of the town centre can just be made out. The doorway seen in this view gave access to the smoke room, part of the interior of which can be seen on the next page. The machine - made bricks are a clue that the building was of no great age and it turns out to have been built in 1899/1900 replacing an earlier pub that stood on the same site and carried the same name.

Above, part of the smoke room which was located on the ground floor, note the electric light, it is known that the Fish & Dolphin was fitted throughout with electricity. This was probably a feature quite rare in Carlisle's late Victorian/ Edwardian pubs. Below, the upstairs room on the first floor, a very small bar is fitted and 2 stoneware spirit barrels can just be made out. There are also two triangular stoneware match strikers on the tables in the foreground.

FISH AND DOLPHIN

As stated, this pub dated to about 1900, but there had been an earlier licensed property standing on this site which also carried the Fish and Dolphin name and that was first recorded in 1844. It is also known that this earlier pub had spells of trading under different signs or names as at circa 1865 it was known as the Woolpack and around 1873 as the Drove, though at the time of its demolition around 1898/99 it was back as the Fish & Dolphin.

By 1900, Jennings the Cockermouth brewers, were in possession of a brand new pub and as can be seen from this interior photograph it was rather smart and was fitted out with good quality furnishings. In fact this view is not what one would have expected of the interior of a Carlisle Victorian pub and the whole scene looks like the sitting-room of a private house of the period, or even a gentleman's club room. It is a great pity that pre-1916 photos of Carlisle pub interiors are so rare, as only this pub and the Crown Hotel in Botchergate can be used as a guide. The quality of the design and fittings seen here in the Fish & Dolphin would probably have been the exception rather than the rule. The class of customers in the district where the pub was located and age of a pub would influence the type of interior layout and fittings and almost certainly one would not have found this type of décor or furnishings in the working-class back-street pubs of 'Wapping' for example. There spittoons and sawdust would have been more likely to be encountered. We know that in the case of the Fish and Dolphin, Jennings were aiming at a 'good front street trade from the business part of the city' (i.e. probably clerks from the city's offices and shops) and a more 'respectable working - class trade,' in other words a more refined and slightly more affluent customer..

The view on this page and that on the bottom of the previous page show the first floor. It is possible that this room was not normally open to customers, possibly being kept as a sort of 'best room' when the pub was holding functions. Judging by these photographs it would have seemed the Fish and Dolphin would have easily met with the coming State Management standards. However it never made it to the State takeover as it was closed by the city magistrates at a licensing session in March 1913. The records relating to this incident give no explanation for how the magistrates arrived at this decision and, though Jennings would have received compensation for the loss of their pub, this judgement surely must have been unexpected.

LOWTHER ARMS

The *Carlisle Patriot* newspaper of the 18 December 1811 mentions a Lowther Arms located in St Cuthbert's lane, but it is not certain whether it was the same property as the building being considered here. What we do know is that this property, illustrated above, carried the name Shakespeare Tavern from circa 1839 to 1857 when, in that year, it had a name change to the Lowther Arms. The above is an architect's elevation showing the Lowther Arms, as it looked in 1904. By this date we know that the property had undergone alterations and in 1907 these were described as to have caused the house to have been 'practically rebuilt.' This expression rebuilt was used more than once in old references to some of Carlisle's pubs and is misleading as it suggests that the existing property on the site was demolished for an entirely new building. In reality this was not always the case and this can be shown here with the Lowther Arms, as at the 1913 licensing sessions it was said the 'front of the house was old.' The interior though had definitely seen considerable structural alterations by 1904 with the addition of a large horseshoe-shaped bar. To fit this in the staircase had been removed and a dividing internal wall taken out. The result was a modernised open-plan layout,but the loss of the staircase meant there was now no easy access to the upper floor and this must have been the reason why the publican did not to live on the premises, as it was described as a 'lock- up bar' in 1907. During this Edwardian period the Maryport Brewery Co owned the pub. There were objections to the house keeping its licence on the grounds that two smoke rooms or 'snugs' forming part of the rear of the building were difficult to supervise by the police. To get to these rooms the law had to go along a passage forty one feet in length(accessed by the door arrowed in the illustration).The pub was to survive these complaints but was closed by the magistrates at a later licensing session in either 1914 or 1915.

SHAKESPEARE TAVERN

The exterior façade of this property with its pedimented entrance suggests a late 18th century date for the building though at that time it may not have been a public house. The earliest record found for it as a licensed property is 1828 when it was known as the Robert Burns Tavern, the street number in 1834 being 5 St Cuthbert's lane. The pub traded under this name or sign up to circa 1839, but it then disappears, (presumably, after this date it must have been trading under a different name the exact identification of which, is not clear). Then in late 1857 the pub was named as the Shakespeare Tavern. However, and rather confusingly, this was adopted from the licensed property that stood exactly opposite which was renamed the Lowther Arms. In 1894 the Shakespeare was owned by the Carlisle Old Brewery Co and it went on to be the last survivor of the St Cuthbert's lane pubs (there had been as many as 8 public houses in the lane in 1855). The State Management actually kept it open as it was still there in 1920, but the extension of the adjoining tall building on the pub's left, then known as Robinson's stores (later to become part of the Binns site), brought about the pubs demolition during the decade 1920-30. The above view of the Shakespeare was taken between 1913 and 1916 when James Allison was the tenant.

FARMERS ARMS

Robert Lockerbie took over the licence on the 4 June 1901 and it is almost certainly him and his wife who are seen in this view. The history of the property as the Farmers Arms can be traced back to between 1852-1855 when it acquired a beerhouse license and, as such, it remained open until spring 1906. The pub was a 'Freehouse' (i.e. not owned by a brewery) and at the time of this view the pub was offering McEwans ales. Strangely considering Carlisle's border location it seems Scotch beers were not widely offered in the city's pubs during the1894-1916 era. The pub's title is explained by it being a popular resort of farmers who frequently came into Carlisle to attend nearby markets and it was called the 'Farmers Inn' as early as 1858. An alternative, though less likely reason, for the pubs naming, could be that the property is known to have possessed a cow shed located in the yard at the rear, but this was closed in 1899 when the Carlisle sanitary authority prohibited its further use.

SPORTSMAN INN

This building (though looking slightly different from this view of around 1901) survives as one of the few historical pubs left in Carlisle's city centre. However it has not always been called the Sportsman, as like many other licensed properties that stood in Carlisle in 1894 it had carried different names during its earlier history. From at least 1770 it was called the Guy Earl Of Warwick (he was a mythical sort of Robin Hood character). Now uncommon as a pub name it was, however, more popular in the past and this name was in use as an English inn sign from at least the 17th century. But its use as a traditional pub name was not the only reason why the title became linked to this property. The publican and owner of this building in 1770 was called Thomas Head (the lane is still known as Heads'), but his wife's maiden name was Warwick and they even named their son Guy when he was born in 1760. In the light of these facts it is obvious just how convenient a name this was for their pub. The first record found for the pub as the Sportsman is 1833, the trail of this name then disappears from the Carlisle street directories for the next 20 years. We know that it had a spell as the Golden Quoit and this name was definitely in use in 1852. Then in 1855 it was back to the Sportsman and it has retained this name ever since. Changes to Head's Lane mean the pub did not occupy the corner site as it does today. A corner property next to the pub was demolished soon after the State takeover.

LORD BROUGHAM

A view of the Lord Brougham taken about 1902. The pub was located on the corner of Crosby Street and Warwick Road (top end then called Henry Street see map) and it was owned by the Carlisle Old Brewery Co. William Hayton was the manager having taken over the licence on the 5 March 1900.

The first record for the 'Lord Brougham' is as a beerhouse in 1837 when a Thomas Carr is recorded as licensee. The pub must have just been recently established by that date as the property itself dates to around the construction of the Turnpike road to Warwick, which commenced in 1830. Lord Brougham was a contemporary political figure at the time of the pub's construction. He was originally from Brougham Hall near Penrith and he rose through various legal and government appointments to become Lord Chancellor. He became a national hero for his successful defence of Queen Caroline, wife of George IV, on charges of adultery. Pubs throughout the country were named after him.

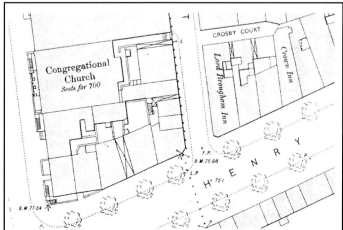

There could also have been a link in the naming of the pub to the 1830 Beerhouse Act, as Lord Brougham had been a proponent of the original scheme. The pub was closed by the State Management in 1932 so as to concentrate trade at the 'Crescent', which opened shortly afterwards. The Lord Brougham still stands but is now a restaurant.

HOWARD ARMS

The history of this building as a public house goes back to 1854/55 when the Howard Arms is listed in the street directory for that year. At the time of writing no earlier reference has been found for the pub. However, the property could have been built as early as 1814, this being the date that Lowther Street began to be laid out as the first new street in the eastern extension of the city after the demolition of the old East Walls. If circa 1814 is the date for the building, there is no evidence that it was in use as a pub trading under another name as there seems to have been no licensed houses in Lowther street at all during the period 1814 -1847. The first pub that seems to have opened on the street was called the White Lion this started to trade around 1849 but was demolished later in the 19th century for new buildings at the junction of Devonshire street. The next pub to be established was the afore mentioned Howard Arms, finally followed by the Apple Tree which started trading during the 1860s, although the property was replaced during state management days by a Redfearn designed building.

 Returning to the subject of the Howard Arms. The green Royal Doulton exterior advertising tiles which have provided a colourful and inviting display in recent years (they had been covered over before 1978) are a late Victorian addition to the pub dating to sometime after 1895. At this time Sir Richard Hodgsons Carlisle Old Brewery bought the pub for £2,800 from a Mr Edward Thompson, who had previously been the publican and also owner. The reason why we can link the ceramic advertising tiles to this Carlisle brewery is that their name, along with that of the Howard Arms, is carried on the same design of tiles, which are still in situ lying beneath the narrow strip of modern board, which advertises 'Traditional Fine Ales', seen in the photograph.

RICKERGATE AREA

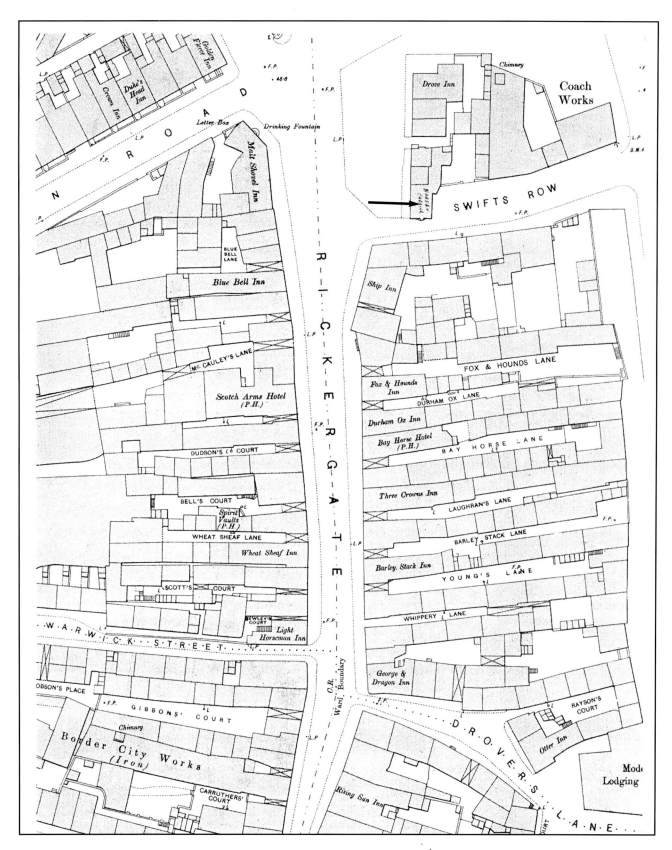

I remember once getting into discussion with a couple of Carlisle 'old timers' on the subject of long gone city pubs, inevitably the 'Gaol Tap' was recollected, but also the *number of pubs that were once located in Rickergate, 'You could swing out of one into another next door.' reminisced one of them. The above Ordnance Survey map for 1899 shows that comment was not far from the truth. This map shows all the full licensed pubs, the property marked by the arrow is the Horse and Farrier beerhouse. Also shown is a unnamed public house in Bells Court marked as a Spirit Vaults. The wine and spirit firm of Steel and Tully occupied it in 1894, but by 1901 the Brampton Old Brewery were supplying the beer.

*see temperance newspaper article on page 124

RISING SUN

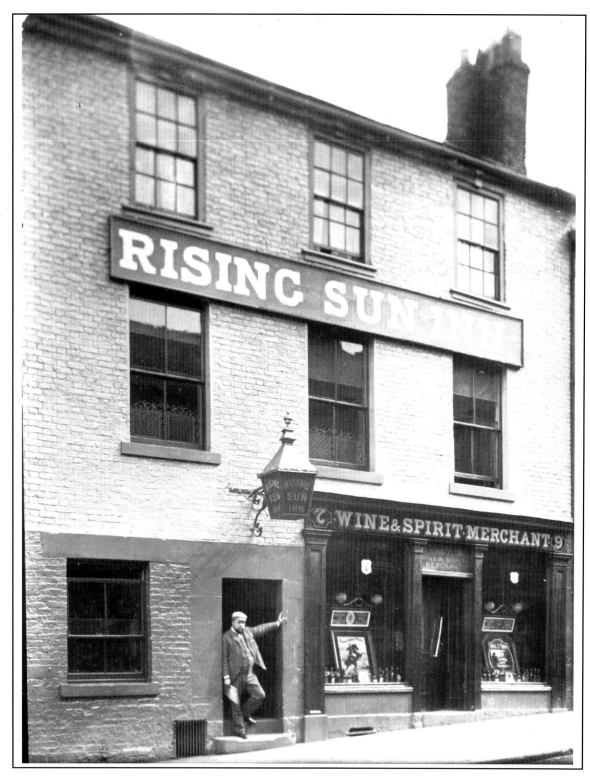

A view of the pub pre-September 1901, up to this date, an R Nish Thom was licensee having taken over from his brother J N Thom in 1891 and the property was owned by the Carlisle Old Brewery Co from 1882, the Rising Sun then being listed at 7 & 9 Scotch Street, but in earlier years it was referred to as Rickergate Brow. The property licensed as the Rising Sun must have gone back to at least 1808 as the *Carlisle Journal* 29.1.1858 said the premises had been well known for more than 50 years. The same paper for 1817 briefly refers to the pub, the licensee then being a James Gilkerson and he was still manager of the Rising Sun in 1829. Then comes a vague period for references to the pub as its name disappears from the street directories of 1837-1847. This suggests the pub has had a name change, but if so it has not been traceable. However, the Rising Sun returns to the listings for 1855 and from then on is regularly indicated in the street directories until its closure in 1906, the cause of this demise being contributed to by accusations that it was a 'den of thieves'. It is of note that when this block of property was demolished for the intended Labour Exchange building the *Carlisle Journal* reported 10.1.1930 that a human skull was unearthed from the backyard of the former pub. The site of the Rising Sun is now under the Debenhams development.

DURHAM OX

The Durham Ox was situated between the Fox and Hounds to its left and a small hotel called the Bay Horse on its right (see map p 105). The above view is an architect's elevation, which dates to 1908. There are photographs showing this block of property pre-demolition in 1961, but the building had been structurally altered by then when compared to the above view. This means we can rely on the above as to showing the original façade of the pub.

The explanation of the pub's name is interesting. The Durham Ox was a shorthorn, the offspring of a common cow and a famous bull called 'Favourite.' At five years old the Durham Ox weighed 216 stones. In February 1801 a Mr Bulmer of Harmby near Bedale built a wagon for the ox and showed him for five weeks. The beast was then sold to a Mr Day of Rotherham. By this time the animal's fame had spread and Mr Day continued to show him in towns all over the country, including Carlisle in 1804. The tour of the ox continued until February 1807 when the animal dislocated a hipbone and had to be slaughtered. Several pubs in Durham and North Yorks were named after him and the above Carlisle pub. The earliest reference found for the Rickergate, Durham Ox, is 1822. However, between 1847 to 1857 the pub had a name change to the *Coachmakers Arms, but in 1858 it reverted to its original name and as such it remained open until 1908/09. *The Carlisle Journal* 17 December 1909 indicates it was definitely closed by the year's end, 'Late Durham Ox, Rickergate Carlisle Old Brewery Co to sell'.

*see newspaper cutting/advert on page 117.

FOX AND HOUNDS

Above, an artist's (Lewis Oswald) illustration of the Fox and Hounds, as seen just prior to its closure in 1960. Even in 1899 the pub was regarded as having some antiquity, being described in a *Carlisle Journal* sales advert as, 'one of the oldest licensed houses in Carlisle.' This was confirmed years later at the time the pub closed, being the last survivor of Rickergate's original pubs its closure was covered by the local press. In this article the State Management revealed that they held deeds for the property that dated back to 1722. During the 1890's the pub was owned by the Carlisle New Brewery, however, probably too much competition from other pubs in the vicinity was the reason why they put the property up for sale during 1899. In the advert the pub's address is given as 25 Rickergate, the tenant and pub manager then being a James Clarke (see bottle p.138). However despite having a 'large bar, comfortable snug and good cellars' it failed to sell. The single-storied building with the green door, being used as an extension to the Fox and Hounds, was in fact the remains of the Durham Ox. This can be compared to the elevation on the previous page and, as can be seen, considerable structural alteration has taken place. This must have occurred at some time after 1908. All the property in the view above was pulled down in 1961 to make way for the Civic Centre.

HORSE AND FARRIER 11 RICKERGATE

These very old properties were numbers 9, Sproats the cloggers and 11 the Horse and Farrier beerhouse, (see map p105). The earliest record for it named the Horse and Farrier is 1829. These views date between 1894 and September 1898, as R. Ridley gave up the licence on the 5th September and Sproats the clog makers moved into number 9 sometime between 1894-97. The pub closed in 1906. Note that the pub's name is not displayed on the property. As referred to elsewhere in this book these circumstances are often connected to a pub being occupied by a wine and spirit merchant, but this was not the case with this particular property. For some reason over the years there seems to have been a tendency to play down the original Horse and Farrier name and it is more frequently encountered in the street directories and licensing registers as just 11 Rickergate.

DROVE INN

The Minns' collection of Carlisle public house photos run to some 30 views and, as referred to previously in this book, most can be dated to around 1901/02. However, there are five that likely date earlier than this, and the above is one of them. The name of the licensee shown on the board is William Hall. The Carlisle licensing register shows that he was the manager from November 1893 to September 1894; a Mary Graham then took over for the next three months followed by John Baxter from December 1894 to 1908. The laws regulating public house licensing and management in the city were strictly maintained by the magistrates and police, also publicans had to re-apply for their licenses annually. Keeping this in mind, it seems highly unlikely that the licensing board on the front of this pub would have been allowed to get out of date by 7 years. This view then dates more likely to 1894. It possibly shows the change over period with the new licensee Mary Graham standing in the doorway.

Above the board is a nicely detailed painted sign showing a gent on a white horse driving cattle. A second and what appears to be a different view is fitted to the gable wall. There is some detail known about one of these signs, firstly the *Carlisle Journal* reported 24 October 1893, 'Drove Inn sign a good one now disappeared,' then on the 9 January 1894 a correspondent to the *Carlisle Journal* from Glasgow, writing on the subject of Carlisle Inn signs, which he remembered fitted to pubs in earlier years, mentioned the sign of the Drove, formerly kept by the late Mrs Darling, and for whom he thought it was painted; the artist being the late Tom Baxter, painter of Scotch Street. Presumably by the date of the above photo this original sign had been recovered. Its final fate though, like a handful of other painted pictorial boards that still hung on the Carlisle pubs during the 1894-1916 period, remains unknown. It has to be said that the affects of weathering would have made it difficult to have preserved these sign boards.

The date of the property is no earlier than 1842 as it is not shown on Studholme's map of Carlisle for that year. However it was built by 1844, being listed as the 'Drove' in the street directory for that year. The name Eleanor Darling was given as the licensee, though the address is given as Eden-Bridge End not Rickergate. By 1872 Iredale's Brewery owned the pub and it remained their property until the State takeover in 1916. The pub was closed by April 1919 and the tower of the Civic Centre now covers this site.

GOLDEN FLEECE

The exact date of this view is not known, all that can be said is that it must have been taken between 1907 (this was the date David Maher took over the licence) and the State takeover in 1916. It was during this period that Maher was regularly part of the Carlisle United football team.

The property dates to the building of Corporation Road, between 1843 to 1849, and it became a public house about 1847, when a John Bulman is listed as licensee of a beerhouse. This is identified in the following street directory for 1852, when the pub is named as the Buck. Then at some time between 1855 and 1858 the pub was closed as the 1858 directory lists a Charles Wright who was a grocer at 1 Corporation Road. Then, surprisingly, just three years later the property returns as a pub when a Stephen Sharp is listed in the Carlisle street directory for1861, the sign being now given as the Golden Fleece, 1 Corporation Road. By 1890 the pub was the property of Trimble's Dalston brewery. However, from 1894 to at least 1911, it was leased to the Maryport Brewery Co and their trademark (badge) appears in the view above. Between January and June 1911 the said brewery delivered 76 barrels of Mild Ale and 16 barrels of India Pale Beer. The State takeover did not immediately have an affect on the pub and it remained open until the new Redfern-designed Malt Shovel opened opposite in 1928. The property still stands and is occupied by a hairdresser.

DUKES HEAD

The view above of the Dukes Head, like that of the original Jovial Sailor on page 35 of this book, is rather blurred. The reason for this is that they have been copied from 1952 reproductions in editions of the *Cumberland Evening News*. The whereabouts of the original photographs used by the newspaper back in 1952 are not known and it seems likely they no longer exist (If any reader can shed any light on what happened to these original photographs then I would be grateful). The above view was taken between 1894 and 1901, when Ann Johnson was the owner and licensee. The earliest definite reference to the Dukes Head is 1858 when an Isaac Graham is listed as an innkeeper at 4 Corporation Road and also trading as a cab proprietor. The pub was a pre-State closure, losing its license sometime between 1902 and 1905.

All three of Corporation Road's 1890s pubs are seen in this modern view taken in 1992. The property marked by the arrow was the Dukes Head, its façade has been rendered since the old view was taken. The property to the left of the arrow was the Crown, which got its license about 1855 and was closed by the State on the 17 September 1916 and the end property at the far right was the Golden Fleece.

MALT SHOVEL

The view above dates sometime between 1894 and 1899. This dating clue is not from the Malt Shovel itself but from the property to the right of the group of men. This is the Golden Fleece and just visible in the photograph is the licensing board carrying the letters J M, the rest of the licensees name is out of view. However, by consulting street directories the licensee is revealed as John Mark Bell. He was in the Golden Fleece in 1897, but not before 1894 as the licensee then of the Golden Fleece was a D Glendinning. The Malt Shovel is interesting in that pre May 1894 it was the property of Carlisle City Council. They sold the pub off in the spring of 1894 to the Workington Brewery for £2,000. The sale was to raise additional funds towards the cost of the Tullie House library and museum development.

The photo right shows a different aspect of the property and was probably taken in 1926/27 just before all of the old Malt Shovel was demolished and replaced by the Redfern designed pub that stands on the same site. Note the drinking fountain built into the wall, this dated from 1855 and was fitted with a chained cup (this is now in Court Square).The earliest reference to the pub is connected to the poet and writer Robbie Burns as it is generally accepted that he stayed at the Malt Shovel in 1787. Before 1893 the Malt Shovel had displayed a pictorial sign showing the figure of a wrestler, G Armstrong.It is not known whether he appeared in portrait or as the model for the maltster holding the shovel. The sign was painted by the Carlisle artist Matthew Nutter and was described by the *Carlisle Journal* 24 October 1893 as a 'good one but now disappeared'.

BLUE BELL HOTEL

A few doors up Rickergate from the Malt Shovel was the Blue Bell. Today it would be opposite the Civic Centre on a site occupied by the Magistrates Court. Through the arch on the right was Blue Bell lane which led to a skittle alley and a quoiting patch, which, along with stabling, were all the property of the pub. Joseph Black was the licensee from the 4 March 1901 and this photograph was probably taken in 1902. The earliest reference for the property named as the Blue Bell is 1822. The pub was taken over by the State in August 1916 and closed in April 1917, because there were just too many licensed properties in Rickergate.

SCOTCH ARMS

The McCauley's were the owners of the Scotch Arms and it is known that they leased out the property to the Wigton Brewery Co for ten years from May 1895. The Wigton brewery had once owned the Scotch Arms in 1783 and this gives us an early date for this Rickergate pub. The following advert appeared in the *Cumberland Pacquet* newspaper for the 15 July 1783; 'To be sold by the Wigton Brewery Co, all that commodious Inn sited in Rickergate known by the name Scotch Arms, being mostly newly built and in very good repair.' This advert implies that the pub was built around 1780. However, this assumption could be misleading, as it is known that other Carlisle pubs referred to as newly built turned out to be as much as twenty years older than the time of the reference. The Scotch Arms could in fact date to around 1763. It is probably Dennis McCauley in the above view and his association with the pub began in the early 1870's .It was during this decade that he pioneered and established Carlisle's first music hall, known as the *Star which was located at the rear of the Scotch Arms. It was said to be a great attraction when first opened, even attracting top stage performers from the London music halls, but by the late 1890's competition from larger modern music halls and even the introduction of the cinematograph at the public hall from 1896 reduced the Star's popularity and it closed in 1899. The Scotch Arms remained open until the 23 October 1916.
*see bottle on page 140.

LIGHT HORSEMAN

As the license for the Light Horseman was discontinued (i.e. causing the pubs closure) on the 3 September 1900, then the above view must be before that date. It is likely that this photo was specifically taken to record this old Rickergate property before closure, as it was realised even by the summer of 1899 that the pub's days were numbered. The cause of this was the intended construction of the new Linton Holme hotel to be sited at Lindisfarne Street. The owners of this building plot also owned the Light Horseman and as the Carlisle magistrates were reluctant to grant new licenses it was planned to sacrifice the 'Horseman' and transfer the license to the new 'Lint' when it was built. The Light Horseman can be traced back to 1829,but there is some evidence to suggest that pre this date it carried different names, these were 1822-26 as the 'Letters'(the meaning of this name is likely an alternative for a 'Board' pub) and 1827-29 as the 'Keg'. The belief that the Letters and Keg are the same property as the Light Horseman has been reached after close study of licensing registers and street directories. As to the date of the building, then remarkably the property appears to date to 1683, as this year is carried on the lintel stone above the far right entrance.

RICKERGATE PUBS IN 1894

The following is a list of all the named public houses located in this area in 1894. Those highlighted in bold have been covered in some detail. The total number of pubs sited in this area in 1894 was actually 20, but as the pub in Bell's Court was an un- named spirit vaults, then it has been omitted from the list.

1.	**RISING SUN**	CLOSED 1906
2.	OTTER INN	CLOSED 1906
3.	GEORGE & DRAGON	CLOSED 27.2.1903
4.	BARLEY STACK	CLOSED 27.2.1903
5.	3 CROWNS INN	CLOSED 18.4.1916
6.	BAY HORSE HOTEL	CLOSED 19.10.1916
7.	**DURHAM OX**	CLOSED 1908/09
8.	**FOX & HOUNDS**	CLOSED 1960
9.	SHIP INN	CLOSED 1906
10.	**HORSE & FARRIER**	CLOSED 1906
11.	**DROVE**	CLOSED APRIL 1917
12.	**GOLDEN FLEECE**	CLOSED 1928
13.	**DUKES HEAD**	CLOSED CIRCA 1904
14.	CROWN	CLOSED 17.9.1916
15.	**MALT SHOVEL**	CLOSED 1927
16.	**BLUE BELL**	CLOSED APRIL 1917
17.	**SCOTCH ARMS**	CLOSED 23.10.1916
18.	WHEAT SHEAF	CLOSED 11.10.1916
19.	**LIGHT HORSEMAN**	CLOSED 3.9.1900

COACHMAKERS' ARMS INN,
(FORMERLY "DURHAM OX"), RICKERGATE, CARLISLE.

SALE OF EXCELLENT HOUSEHOLD FURNITURE, PUBLIC HOUSE REQUISITES, & OTHER EFFECTS,
Without the slightest reservation.

MR. WILLIAM BROWNE has received instructions to SELL, by AUCTION, on TUESDAY next, SEPTEMBER 2nd, 1856, at One o'Clock in the Afternoon, on the Premises of Mr. JOSHUA OGLETHORPE, Innkeeper, RICKERGATE, CARLISLE, (who is about to leave this country for New South Wales), all his very substantial and useful HOUSEHOLD FURNITURE, SPIRIT BAR and PUBLIC HOUSE REQUISITES, and EFFECTS.—Particulars in Bills of the day. Also, Coachmakers' Wheel Pit, Coach Sets, Paint Stone, Mullers and Knives; also, about 500lb weight of White Lead, Red, Green, Black, and other Coloured Paints, suitable f r Cartwrights, Machine Makers, and Farm Implements generally, the whole put up in suitable lots.

Above, this advert appeared in the *Carlisle Journal* newspaper on the 29 August 1856.

Left, the Fox and Hounds and what had been the Durham Ox are seen in this view about 1959/60. The original roof line of the Durham Ox (marked by an arrow) before it was altered can just be made out on the gable end brickwork of what had been the Bay Horse hotel.

SOME PUBS ON
THE CITY OUTSKIRTS

THE BEEHIVE

Above, a recent view of the pub taken in 1996, the flat roofed entrance building is of modern construction. The taller building behind with the creeping ivy attached is the original Beehive pub, the lower red brick building running parallel with the lane was built onto it in 1899/1900(see plans that date to November 1899 on next page).

The original Beehive was built sometime between 1849-1864 and the first reference to it as a pub can be found in the 1872 licensing register, it then being occupied by a Robert Irving but owned by Iredale's brewery. The pub seems to have started out with a 'Full' license but in later years it was relegated to a beerhouse 'on' license. The Beehive had up to around 1917 (when it was closed by the State Management) a nearby rival in the Petteril Bridge Inn. This building now occupied as a private dwelling stands more or less opposite the Beehive and can still be recognised for what it once was as its faded name can just be made out painted onto its gable. This property was slightly earlier than the Beehive, as it can be traced back to 1855.

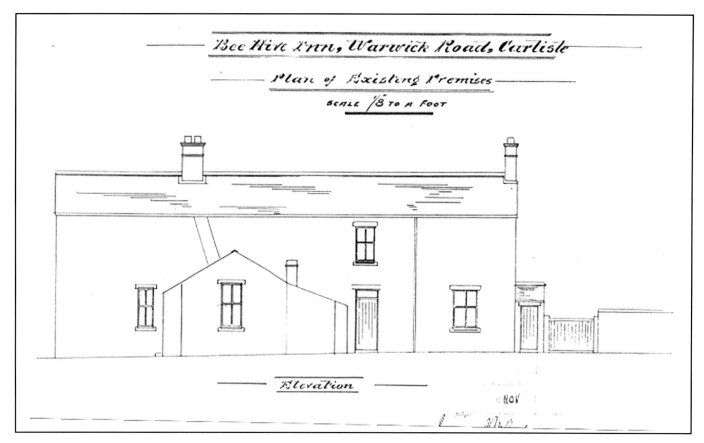

Above, the Beehive as it would have looked from the adjacent lane pre-1900. It seems likely that the building pre 1872 was originally a farmhouse. Interior plans for the ground floor of the above building show that the pub was then not fitted out with a bar. Instead the property was divided into Smoke Rooms and Parlours and it seems that customers must have been waited on, the beer being tapped off the barrel instead of the more efficient method of delivery via a 'beer engine'. This situation would change when the new structure seen on the elevation below was added in 1900. This building according to the plans had a 21 foot bar fitted and cellarage which was about 6 -7 foot deep. This cellar was accessed via a trap located behind the bar and is presumably still in use.

CURROCK HOTEL

On the 24 June 1898 the brewers Samuel Allsopps of Burton-Upon-Trent had their plan for a hotel to be sited at Boundary Road approved by the building inspectors. By August 1899 the hotel was built, but building it was one thing, selling drink in it was to be another. It would seem that Allsopps had gone ahead and put up the property without at first securing a drink licence but, as the property had been built as a hotel it was probably thought it stood a better chance of being approved by the licensing magistrates. However, Carlisle had a strong temperance movement particularly during the 1890's and they put up an effective resistance to the 'Currock'. This began on the 1 September 1899 just three days before the Carlisle annual licensing sessions when it was expected that the property would get its license.

The opposition was brought together at a large meeting held at Goodwin school, presided over by the Reverend Lonsdale, and said to be quote: 'a largely attended meeting, to protest against a license being granted to Allsopps so that they could sell intoxicating liquor in the large premises which they have caused to be erected in Boundary Terrace.' The chairman mentioned that 'many thrifty working men had recently purchased houses in that district and it was rather hard on them that after they had expected they were going to reside permanently in this hitherto quiet district to have a public house thrust into their midst. It had been stated on behalf of Allsopps that the premises were to be an hotel, but if anybody examined the building they would see there was going to be one long bar. If a licence was granted to this place it would have the most demoralising effect on the district.' It was pointed out by a Mr Martin of Gardenia Street that the public house would be a temptation to the many railway men who lived there and a menace to the safety of the travelling public. It was also said 'That this meeting emphatically protests against any increase in the number of licenses in the Boundary Terrace and Currock districts.' This statement seems odd and must refer to 'off' licenses as there were no other public houses in this area of Carlisle. A reverend Boyd then spoke on the evils of drink and its affect on society and a petition against the pub was laid on the table at this meeting and it was signed by 250 inhabitants of the district. This meeting had the desired effect on the magistrates and the licence was refused. In 1900 Allsopps tried again but the opposition was still as strong, the vicar of Upperby saying 'a bar and nothing but a bar, the place would become a perfect pandemonium' and the licence was blocked a second time. The Currock Hotel did not open until 1903 when it finally got its licence, but by now Allsopps had sold the property to Jennings brewery. If some of the locals weren't keen patrons in these early years then there were always others looking for a few pints and the Currock became popular with railwaymen from the nearby Upperby sheds and yard. The above view was taken about 1987 when Greenhall Whitley supplied the beer.

GREEN DRAGON

Above, this view of the Green Dragon was taken in 1990, but the angle of the photo well illustrates the development of this old pub. The earliest reference found for the Green Dragon is an advert in the Carlisle Journal newspaper for 1806, when a William Underwood was proprietor. However the property was enlarged in 1860 with the building of an extension forward to Newtown Road (this later development I have indicated with a line). The gable end of what is the earlier original Green Dragon is indicated by the arrow.

In 1904 the Carlisle New Brewery acquired the pub and it was to remain open for some time not closing until 1999/2000. However, it was at the original smaller Green Dragon in 1847 that took place one of the most unusual events known to have been linked to a Carlisle pub. This somewhat sad tale was recalled in the 'Local Jottings' column of the *Carlisle Journal* of the 12 October 1899 and is given here.

Last week in recalling the appearance of a lady in "Bloomer" costume at the Green Dragon Inn at Newtown, I mentioned the existence of a small menagerie in the gardens of the inn, a bear being among the animals exhibited. There is a tale connected with that bear. It was a North American grisly, and was chained to a tree in an unenclosed space behind the monkey cages. On Friday evening, September 3rd, 1847, a man named William Rawson, a porter with Mr. Bonnell, soda water manufacturer, called at the inn in the way of his business, and went into the garden to see the bear, and to give it some bread, as had been his wont on several occasions. He was accompanied by an old man of the name of Gass. Rawson held out some crumbs of bread to the bear, which it took quietly from his hand. He then offered his hand without bread, when the bear, with both its fore paws, suddenly seized him by the arm, and dragged him within its circle, throwing him down, and instantly commencing to worry him. The old man Gass, who was 79 years of age, courageously seized the infuriated animal by the collar, and Mrs. Cowen, wife of the landlord of the inn, got hold of its chain ; but both their efforts proved ineffectual to relieve the unfortunate sufferer. Two men speedily arrived with pitchforks and succeeded in forcing off the bear and dragging the man from within its reach. It made no attempt to turn upon its assailants. Rawson was found to be dreadfully lacerated about the head, neck, and shoulders, and was immediately removed to the Infirmary, where he died on the following Monday morning. The bear was shot on Saturday morning by Mr. Cowen. At that time people used pomatum for the hair a great deal more than they do now, and the favourite and most expensive unguent was "bear's grease." I remember that after the Newtown bear was killed Mr. Carruthers, the hairdresser, whose shop was at the top of Castle Street, created what we nowadays call a "boom" in bear's grease by announcing that he could supply the real genuine "bear's grease" from the "grisly" in question.

NORTH BRITISH RAILWAY INN

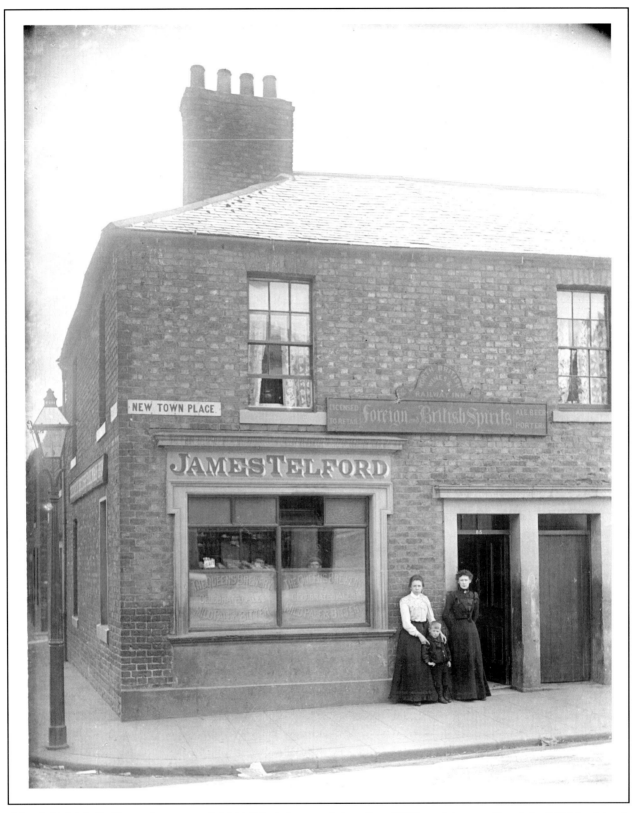

The North British Railway Inn around 1901/02, it is certainly after 1900 as this was the date J.Telford took over the licence. The pub still stands but underwent structural alterations about 1920. Sited on the corner of Bright Street and New Town Place, this block is known to have been built between 1842-1848,but there seems to be no record of it being a licensed property until 1861 when a Robert Dawson had a beerhouse on Newtown Place. Then in 1869, the street directory lists the pub as the Pedestrian Arms and it seems it didn't acquire the North British name until around 1877. The significance of the latter naming is linked to the Scottish railway company of the same title who had locomotive sheds and yard not far away, which were accessed from 'Engine Lonning.' By the 1890's the pub had been acquired by Grahams Queens brewery and their advertising can be made out in the above view. When the State took over the city's pubs in 1916 they reverted its name to the Pedestrian Arms. It is not known why the pub acquired this title in the first place and the actions by the State Management also seem odd as the North British Railway Company was still operating at that time.

CARLISLE TEMPERANCE
VERSUS THE LOCAL DRINKS TRADE

Above, a superb view of the 'Gaol Tap' taken in 1897 at the time of Queen Victoria's Diamond Jubilee celebrations.

Temperance societies were a national movement in Victorian Britain and they were very much to the fore in Carlisle during the 1890's. The following is extracted from a newspaper report that appeared in the *Carlisle Journal* on Friday the 1 September 1899. It covers a meeting that was held by the local temperance party to which it seems some of the city's publicans and members of the Carlisle Licensed Victuallers Society were invited to attend. As it turned out the temperance supporters probably regretted this decision because of the hecklers. This meeting is not printed here in its entirety as only those parts of the article where reference is made to some of the city's pubs is relevant. The best words spoken at this meeting were saved till last as the meeting split up. Here following then are extracts from the meeting;
'Last night what was described as a citizens meeting which had been organised by the Temperance party was held in the Town Hall, to consider the alarming increase in the size of public houses in the city, the number of back doors leading to licensed premises, and the continuance of serving drink to children in defiance of the suggestion of the magistrates at Brewster sessions, and to pass resolutions thereon. There was a large attendance, the hall being quite filled. Amongst those occupying seats on the bench were Mr Robert Watson (Temperance party), the Rev C T Horan, the Rev W G Bird, and Mr W Etchells (proprietor of the *Northern News*). In the body of the hall were Mr T Nicholson (of the Golden Fleece), Mr J Broughton, solicitor to the Licensed Victuallers Association, Mr J Coulthard, secretary of the same association, Mr G Hodgson auctioneer, and many others.
  The chairman (J H Barlow) in opening the meeting, said that it seemed to them that some of the restrictions which had been placed on the liquor traffic by Parliament had not been so carefully observed in Carlisle as they might have been. Publicans were opening side doors and back doors and increasing facilities for drinking which was not desirable. When they found the publican increasing his premises it indicated that his business was prospering, and they knew that the increased sale of drink would lead to increased drunkenness and the crime and misery which followed from it. Why did the publicans want side doors and back entrances? (a voice from the crowd: 'They don't want them' and 'it's the teetotallers that go to the back doors' followed by laughter).'

CARLISLE TEMPERANCE
VERSUS THE LOCAL DRINKS TRADE

'The chairman resuming, said they would be inflicting no hardship on the publicans when they wished to prevent them from selling drink to children of tender years. It was the least they could do to prevent children being brought into contact with mischief, and he could not understand how anybody could send children to public-houses (cheers from the audience). Mr Robert Watson, then moved the first resolution as follows, 'that this meeting of citizens assembled in the town hall, respectfully urge upon the licensing justices the immediate necessity of putting a stop to the further increase in the accommodation for drinking purposes in public-houses throughout the city; and also order the closing of all back and side entrances to the said type of premises as these facilities are a special temptation and render proper police supervision impossible.' He said that last night at seven o'clock he began to explore some of the main streets in the city and some of the lanes leading there from. His first stop was outside the Lord Brougham, Warwick Road, where without let or hindrance some cottages had been added. There were 3 front doors and 1 back door to this pub. Minn's in Lowther street (Apple Tree) had 3 front and 1 back door, whilst the Howard Arms further down the street, had 1 front,1 side and 1 back door.

Language was too poor to describe drink-cursed Rickergate. It reeked with drink dens (cries of 'oh' from the audience), from the Rising Sun to the Malt Shovel, there were more rickety gates thru Rickergate's rickety public houses than in any other part of the city.(Laughter). A commission should be appointed to inquire into the reason why this entrance into Carlisle should be studded so thickly with a battery of liquor shops which did more harm than the Scots who came over once upon a time and stole our cattle (more laughter). He would like to transport every public-house in Rickergate into Chatsworth and Portland Squares for twelve months, and give the poor, drink-tempted wretches a chance to regain their lost man and womanhood, and let the rich see what a nice thing it was to have a lot of public houses in their midst.

Ismay's spirit store at the junction of Scotch Street and East Tower Street had 1 front door and doors on each side round corners north and south - cannons to right, cannons to left and cannons before. (laughter from the audience).

Nanson's Vaults in West Tower Street, had 2 front and 1 back door, the Crown and Anchor (rebuilt) had 3 doors. His next visit was to the 'Klondike'-(laughter)- in Fisher Street, that was 'Klondike' to the owner, not to the customers, this house has at least 4 doors. In St Cuthbert's lane there were three pubs each with 2 doors. Then on to Ferguson's lane where there was a miserable shanty called the Fish (laughter). It must be a very antique fish, it looked like a relic dropped out of Noah's Ark and ought to be carted away to Tullie House museum, minus the liquor. He was sorry for the fish and the fishermen inside, they seldom got a glimpse of the sun; the lane was so narrow that its resplendent glory could not get well within the portals of this abode of Bacchus.

The 'Gaol Tap' had 8 doors, so that if the 'chucker out' was a bad marksman and missed one door he was sure to hit another-(laughter). The Wellington had 2 front and 1 back door, the Victoria Hotel was a big place, going about as far back as from English Street to Lowther Street, with 1 front and 2 side doors, the Red Lion Hotel was another huge concern with 3 front doors and at least 1 back door, while the Caledonian had 3 front, 1 side and a back entrance. The Railway Tavern had been rebuilt and had 2 front and 1 back door. As he stood looking at the back entrance a mite of a girl came out with a jug, he asked her how old she was and she replied 'seven'-(cries of 'Shame!' from the audience), but what were they to expect? Mr John Hunt, a leading man in the Liquor Traffic Defence League, told the publicans not to mind the magistrates but to serve the children who came, even if they could only toddle. The next pub up Botchergate on this side was the Albion, this property was a wonderful invention and had the drapers shop of Mr Irving Bell hemmed in on either side, 1 front door to this pub was in Botchergate, another in Portland Place where a confectioners shop had been swallowed up, the draper was content with 1 door but his next door neighbour the publican wanted 2. The Earl Grey had 3 front and 1 back door and the Samson, where many a man had been shorn of his locks-(laughter)- had 2 front and 2 back doors, the Golden Lion was a monster-(laughter)- and had 5 entrances to its gilded bar, the Crown Hotel was being altered, and already there was a connection to the off sales shop next door, a watchful eye must be kept on this latest enlargement to the domain of drinkdom. The last two houses in the evenings survey beggared description, talk about the Catacombs of Rome!. These pubs were a perfect maze- a labyrinth of ways in and out, Carlisle policemen were very clever in catching respectable tradesmen hanging goods outside their shops and hauling them up to the Town Hall, but the bobbies could be dodged and bamboozled in Botchergate's drink shops, the Hare and Hounds had 2 front doors and 4 up the lane and Ismays Vaults in Collier Lane had 3- a nice place to catch railway men. Forster's (old 'Cumberland') had 2 front and 3 doors down a passage far away from the front street.

He wondered if the licensing justices ever saw these places and knew what they were doing. With all these back doors for weak men and women to sneak into, could they wonder at so many wrecks of humanity? He asked the citizens of Carlisle to rouse from their false security and for the sake of home and country demand an immediate stoppage to any further increase in drinking facilities, and also that these snares of back doors be closed.(cheers).' The Reverend James Hume seconded the motion as representing the Evangelical Free Church Council. He did not believe in back doors, (a voice from the audience 'its where they put their ashes out' followed by laughter). He then resumed, one of the main reasons why publicans want back doors was that drinking was not now regarded as a respectable thing- (a voice 'have

CARLISLE TEMPERANCE
VERSUS THE LOCAL DRINKS TRADE

* Note the reference to 140 licensed houses in Mr Watson's letter is somewhat misleading as he has included some 17 'off' licenses. These properties are known to have been shops, being a mixture of grocers with a beer license and some wine/spirit **shops** and as such they were **not** 'on' licensed public houses.

(continued from previous page):-

you got a back door to your house?' further laughter). The Rev C.T.Horan supported the resolution, he congratulated the meeting on having opposition, because it showed they were stirring them up. He took up the question from the standpoint of the gospel temperance. He did not say that it was absolutely wrong for a man to take a glass of beer or wine-(a voice from the audience 'thanks mate you're a gent' and much Laughter), resuming he said that it was patent to everyone that the public-houses were responsible for the greater part of our national intemperance (followed by 'Hear, hear'). He urged the licensing justices not to grant a public house that was going to be asked for in his parish. They want to bring Rickergate down to their part of the city, but they would sooner Rickergate was left where it was-(loud cheers).

  The Chairman then asked if there was any amendment to the resolution. Mr George Rushfirth (anti-Temperance) then rose amid laughter and said that he proposed the following as an amendment; 'That in the opinion of this meeting the magistrates are the fit and proper persons to judge which back doors or what public houses are entitled to a licence, without the interference of the so called Temperance party.-(laughter and cheers)-resuming he said, when Mr Watson was creeping and crawling about like an evil spirit-(Cheers from the audience) why could he not watch the clubs and tackle the clubs which were a far greater curse and abomination?-(Cheers). When Mr Watson was spying and looking around did he ever see a publican drag a man in and force him to drink?-('No'), How did Mr Watson get his living?'-(cheers and laughter).

Mr Watson's resolution was however put and carried amid loud cheers by an overwhelming majority of the audience. At the end of the meeting the chairman was requested to present copies of the resolution to the licensing justices on the following Monday. As the meeting separated though, one individual shouted out -'Come on, lets all go and have a pint.'

LIST OF CARLISLE 'ON' LICENCES IN 1894

The following is a list of all the properties in Carlisle at this date that possessed a 'ON' licence, i.e. where drink could be legally sold for consumption inside the premises, they range from the large city hotels down to back-street pubs. This list also includes 10 properties which were classed as Spirit Stores at the time, this means these buildings were then occupied by wine and spirit merchants and as referred to elsewhere in this book this often resulted in the publican not displaying a name or sign.

  The total number of 'On' licenses in the city in 1894 runs to exactly 123 and the following list of these properties has been arranged alphabetically.

No	NAME	LOCATION
1	ALBION	BOTCHERGATE
2	ANGEL INN	14-16 ENGLISH STREET
3	ANGLERS ARMS	SHADDONGATE
4	APPLE TREE	LOWTHER STREET
5	BARLEY STACK	RICKERGATE
6	BEE HIVE	WARWICK ROAD
7	BIRD-IN-HAND	CASTLE STREET
8	BAY HORSE	RICKERGATE
9	BLUE BELL	SCOTCH STREET
10	BLUE BELL	RICKERGATE
11	BRICKLAYERS ARMS	CALDEWGATE
12	BOWLING GREEN	LOWTHER STREET
13	BUSH HOTEL	ENGLISH STREET
14	CALEDONIAN	BOTCHERGATE
15	CALEDONIAN INN	ENGLISH DAMSIDE
16	CITY VAULTS	FISHER STREET
17	CITY HOTEL	ENGLISH STREET
18	COACH AND HORSES	BLACKFRIARS STREET
19	COUNTY HOTEL	COURT SQUARE
20	CROWN HOTEL	BOTCHERGATE
21	CROWN INN	HENRY STREET/WARWICK ROAD
22	CROWN INN	CORPORATION ROAD
23	CROWN AND ANCHOR	C&A LANE ENGLISH STREET
24	CROWN AND MITRE HOTEL	ENGLISH STREET
25	CUMBERLAND	BOTCHERGATE
26	CUMBERLAND WRESTLERS ARMS	CURROCK STREET
27	DENTON INN	DENTON HOLME
28	DOG AND BULL	PEASCODS LANE/ENGLISH STREET
29	DROVE	RICKERGATE
30	DUKES HEAD	CORPORATION ROAD
31	DURHAM OX	RICKERGATE
32	DEAKINS VAULTS	BOTCHERGATE
33	EARL GREY	BOTCHERGATE
34	FARMERS ARMS	SAINT CUTHBERTS LANE
35	FISH INN	FERGUSONS LANE/ENGLISH STREET
36	FISH AND DOLPHIN	ST CUTHBERTS LANE
37	FOX AND HOUNDS	RICKERGATE
38	FRIARS TAVERN	DEVONSHIRE STREET
39	GEORGE AND DRAGON	RICKERGATE
40	GLOBE	SCOTCH STREET
41	GLOBE	CALDEWGATE
42	GOLDEN FLEECE	ST NICHOLAS
43	GOLDEN FLEECE	CORPORATION ROAD
44	GOLIATH	CROWN STREET
45	GOLDEN LION	BOTCHERGATE
46	GREAT CENTRAL HOTEL	VICTORIA VIADUCT
47	GREEN DRAGON	NEWTOWN ROAD

48	HARE AND HOUND	BOTCHERGATE
49	HOLE-IN-THE-WALL	ST ALBANS ROW/SCOTCH STREET
50	HORSE AND FARRIER	OLD RAFFLES
51	HORSE AND FARRIER	11 RICKERGATE
52	HOWARD ARMS	LOWTHER STREET
53	JOINERS ARMS	CALDEWGATE
54	JOVIAL SAILOR	CALDEWGATE
55	LIGHT HORSEMAN	RICKERGATE
56	LION AND LAMB	SCOTCH STREET
57	LIVERPOOL ARMS	BEWLEYS COURT/ ENGLISH STREET
58	LONDON & NORTH WESTERN	JAMES STREET
59	LORD BROUGHAM	WARWICK ROAD
60	LORNE ARMS	SHADDONGATE
61	LOWTHER ARMS	ST CUTHBERTS LANE
62	MALT SHOVEL	RICKERGATE
63	MASONS ARMS	SOUTH JOHN STREET
64	MILBOURNE ARMS	MILBOURNE STREET
65	MALTSTERS ARMS	CALDEWGATE
66	MOULDERS ARMS	CURROCK STREET
67	NELSON BRIDGE	DENTON HOLME
68	NEW INN	ENGLISH DAMSIDE
69	NORTHUMBERLAND ARMS	BOTCHERGATE
70	ODDFELLOWS INN	CROWN STREET
71	OLD ANCHOR	CALDEWGATE
72	OLD BUSH	OLD BUSH LANE/SCOTCH STREET
73	OLD BLACK BULL	ANNETWELL STREET
74	OLD KINGS HEAD	FISHER STREET
75	ORDNANCE ARMS	FINKLE STREET
76	OTTER INN	DROVERS LANE/RICKERGATE
77	PEDESTRIAN ARMS	NEWTOWN ROAD
78	PETTERIL BRIDGE INN	WARWICK ROAD
79	PHEASANT	CALDEWGATE
80	PLOUGH	CALDEWGATE
81	PRINCE OF WALES	DENTON STREET
82	QUARTER OF MUTTON	BROWNS LANE/OFF CASTLE ST
83	QUEEN ADELAIDE	BOTCHERGATE
84	QUEENS HEAD INN	CALDEWGATE
85	QUEENS HEAD HOTEL	ST ALBANS ROW
86	RAILWAY HOTEL	LONDON ROAD
87	RAILWAY TAVERN	BOTCHERGATE
88	RED LION HOTEL	BOTCHERGATE
89	RISING SUN	RICKERGATE
90	ROSE AND CROWN	LOWTHIANS LANE/ENGLISH STREET
91	ROYAL OAK	CALDEWGATE
92	SAMSON	LONDON ROAD
93	SARACENS HEAD	ANNETWELL STREET
94	SCOTCH ARMS	RICKERGATE
95	SHAKESPEARE	SAINT CUTHBERTS LANE
96	SHIP INN	RICKERGATE
97	SPINNERS ARMS	MILBOURNE STREET
98	SPORTSMAN	HEADS/ST CUTHBERTS LANE
99	SPREAD EAGLE	LANE OFF ENGLISH STREET
100	SPIRIT STORE/ISMAYS	SCOTCH STREET
101	SPIRIT STORE	ENGLISH STREET

102	SPIRIT STORE/HOPE&BENDLES	LOWTHER STREET
103	SPIRIT STORE A	100-104 ENGLISH STREET
104	SPIRIT STORE B	WEST TOWER STREET
105	SPIRIT STORE	BELLS PLACE/RICKERGATE
106	SPIRIT STORE C	SHADDONGATE
107	SPIRIT STORE D	CASTLE STREET
108	SPIRIT STORE	ST ALBANS ROW
109	SPIRIT STORE/CARRICK&RIDDEL	LOCATION NOT KNOWN
110	THREE CANNONS	THREE CANNONS LANE
111	THREE CROWNS	RICKERGATE
112	THREE CROWNS	ENGLISH STREET
113	TURF HOTEL	SWIFTS
114	UNION HOTEL	CITADEL ROW
115	VICTORIA HOTEL	ENGLISH STREET
116	WAGGON AND HORSES	CALDEWGATE
117	WELLINGTON	ENGLISH STREET
118	WHEAT SHEAF	RICKERGATE
119	WHITE HORSE VAULTS	LANE OFF BLACK FRIARS ST
120	WHITE OX	WOODRUFFE TERRACE
121	WILLIAM JAMES M.P.	WILLOW HOLME
122	WOOLPACK	MILBURN STREET
123	WRESTLERS ARMS	ANNETWELL STREET

Letter A, this was the City Arms/Gaol Tap and Pine Apple, B was Nansons Vaults, C became the Duke Of York in 1896 and D the Board, it seems this title was not displayed on the property until after 1916

100, 102, & 104 English-St.

PUBLIC HOUSE CHECKS
(see colour plate on page 130)

Pub checks are a form of token, usually made of brass or other copper alloy, bearing the name of the public house in which they were used and a value. At their fullest they carry the name of the public house or beer house, the address and town, the name of the licensee, and a value. There are variations on these and not all appear on every check. They are usually well-made and struck for a named pub. A second type, known as a 'poor man's check', uses a stock token with a standard struck obverse such as Queen Victoria's head or a double-headed eagle and a blank reverse. On the blank side a publican would add details of his pub using letter punches. Most of these have a minimum of detail often in the form of initials, which make them very difficult to identify. They are common in Lancashire.

The most common values appearing on checks are ; one penny, penny ha'penny, two penny, two and ha'penny and three penny which correspond to the price of pints and half-pints of beer at different times or different qualities. There is probably no single use for pub checks but they seem to be connected to a form of 'wet rent' or repayment for beer. Groups such as Friendly Societies would meet at a particular public house. Rather than being charged for the use of a room they would pay for a set number of drinks. The members of the society might not want to consume all the drinks on the given night and could defer consumption by making payment for the beer and receiving tokens to be used at a later date. In other cases the checks were similarly used in connection with pub games such as bowling, skittles or bagatelle, and on occasion this could lead to their being used (illegally) for gambling. When a public house had a concert hall attached, the price of admission would included the cost of a drink, given in the form of a check to be redeemed later. Some checks may also have been used as bonus payments paid by companies to workers.

The use of checks flourished in the second half of the 19th century but a few were still in use in the early 20th century. They appear in greatest numbers in the West Midlands, centred on Birmingham where the main token manufacturers were, but at least a few appear in most parts of the country. In Cumbria checks are known in greatest numbers for Carlisle and Kendal with a small number for Penrith and only one for Workington. The lack of checks for Whitehaven, Workington and Maryport is, at first sight, surprising but it may be that seaports saw a more transient clientele who did not have need for checks.

Above, both sides of a check for the Jovial Hatter Inn. It can be dated to 1884 - 1890 when James Hill was the licensee. This pub was located at the end of a short stretch of housing in Wood Street, (see map on page 52) being established there from circa 1854. This terraced housing had at one-time fronted Carrick's hat factory (the firm moved to Norfolk Street by 1878) and this obviously explains the naming of the pub. The Jovial Hatter was closed in 1893.

1. EARL GREY, The check can not be dated because it lacks a licensee's name.
2. FISH INN, Ferguson's lane. The check has the surname Johnson with no Christian name. The license changed hands several times between Thomas and Thomasina Johnson between 1869 and 1886.
3. GLOBE INN, Caldewgate. John Armstrong was licensee circa 1869 - circa 1880.
3a. JOVIAL HATTER, 21 Wood Street. Also called Jolly Hatter, closed 1893
4. QUARTER OF MUTTON, at corner of Brown's Lane and Castle Street, just north of Green Market. Joseph Bulmore was licensee 1863 - 1878. The pub was closed on the 26 September 1898.
5. SPREAD EAGLE, Catherine Harding was licensee circa 1876 - 1884 in succession to John Harding who held the license from the 6th August 1875.
6. SPRING GARDENS (= Bowling Green), corner of Spring Gardens Lane and Lowther Street. George Peascod was licensee Circa 1871 - 1872.
7. BOWLING GREEN HOTEL, the reverse has the countermarked initials A.T. for Andrew Tait, licensee 1886 - 1901. The token may have been first issued earlier.
8. PRINCE OF WALES, 104 Denton Street. Frances Fernley the licensee from 1870 - circa 1880 was the widow of Ralph Fernley the previous owner who died in 1869.
9. PRINCE OF WALES, the reverse has the initials J.R.D. of John Robert Dalton, licensee circa 1880 - 1890 (Mrs Fernley and later Elizabeth Fernley continued to own the Prince of Wales.

(1)

(2)

(3)

(3)

(4)

(5)

(6)

(7)

(8)

(9)

BOTTLED BEER

Countrywide during the 1880's there occurred a very marked increase in the demand for bottled beers and this had reached Carlisle during the 1890's as the local brewers started to increase this line of trade.

Bottling of beer in Britain pre-1880 had taken place, however, much of it was destined for export and less was directed at the home market. The bottling that was carried out in these earlier years tended to be undertaken by specialist bottlers, wine and spirit merchants and grocers and it was seen as a distinct business of its own. However, 20 years later virtually every regional brewer around Britain had incorporated it into the general work of the brewery.

So stated Frank Lott when he presented a paper on the subject of bottled beers to the Institute of Brewing in 1901, and importantly he gives a reason for this, he says "the large increase in the 'tied-house' trade has no doubt been the cause of so many brewers taking up the bottling business".

This occurred around Britain increasingly during the 1885-1900 period and on a smaller scale was undertaken in Carlisle especially during the 1890's as the local brewers bought pubs.

There was another event that caused the big shift towards bottled beers, namely the introduction of the screw stoppered beer bottle. In fact, if the advert below is to be believed, it seems to have been the primary cause for the increase in British bottled beers towards the end of the 19th century.

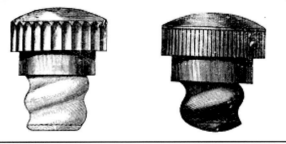

Advert from the Brewers Guardian 11.6.1889

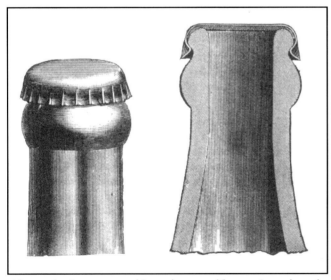

Above the 'crown -cork'was invented by an American in 1892 and was introduced to the British brewing trade in 1895, though it did not come into widespread use here until the early 1950's.

Above, a pottery ash tray decorated with a transfer advert, the item dates to circa 1906. Not all brewers switched to using the screw stopper as the picture shown here is of a bottle closed by the traditional cork. The word 'KREME' was a trade name for their nourishing stout. Jennings supplied about six Carlisle pubs during the 1894 - 1916 period, including the Waggon and Horses and Currock Hotel. These two pubs were lost to them when the State Control took over in 1916.

NEW BOTTLE SEAL.

THE new bottle seal which has met with such marked approval in America is sure to find its way into the favour of bottlers and consumers in the United Kingdom. The bottles have a groove inside the neck, shaped like a mortice joint, into which the seal is forced, assuming an internal arch-shape, so that no matter how strong the internal pressure

How to open

Opened

is, it cannot be removed. The seal has a pure tasteless facing inside, and being only used once, every bottle has a fresh clean stopper, and no rusty wires or balls or screws are present as in some other patents. The accompanying illustrations will enable our readers to see how simple and ingenious this latest American " notion " is.

Despite this up-beat advert of 1890, this type of bottle and stopper does not seem to have caught on in Carlisle as only Hope& Bendle are known to have used it.

Victorian bottled beer had a certain attraction to some of the public, in that generally it was a gassier drink when compared to the fairly flat draught beers of the time, and contemporary references on the subject often comment on the noticeable "sharpness and 'life' so peculiar to bottled beers". That Victorian bottled beer was reasonably charged with carbon dioxide gas was the direct result of the presence of a certain amount of yeast that was left in the beer, bringing about a secondary fermentation in the confines of the bottle itself. There was, however, a slight draw back with this process in that the yeast settled out as dregs forming a deposit at the bottom of the bottle which could be disturbed when the beer was poured out. Some of these deposits were more easily disturbed than others and Stout was more prone to dropping a heavier sediment than Pale Ale.

BOTTLED BEER

At the beginning of this article on bottled beers it was remarked on how Carlisle breweries increased their trade in this line during the 1890's. Printed below is a copy from a Carlisle New Brewery document dating to 1901/02.

Jovial Sailor Two years supply

	Draught				Bottle				Spirit						
	Bls	£	s	d	Doz	£	s	d	Galls	£	s	d	£	s	d
1901 January to December	216 9/18	433	13	9	591	44	15	6	518.5	406	17	3	885	6	6
1902 January to December	217 14	435	14	6	921	67	16	6	629.9	491	0	2	996	11	2
	433 7/18	869	8	3	1512	114	12	0	1148.4	897	17	5	1881	17	0
Weekly average	4 1/6	8	7	2	14 1/2	1	2	6½	11.4	8	12	8	18	1	10½

The bottle column shows 591 dozen bottles(or put another way 591 crates) sold to the publican over the year 1901. The figure is considerably higher for some reason (oddly enough the Carlisle New Brewery Co actually maintained that their beer sales were down throughout Carlisle in 1902 because of the cold summer) the following year with 921 crates going to the pub. The figures fluctuate, but even so the weekly average at this **one** pub was 14 crates a week. Other records for some of the New Brewery's pubs circa 1902, show the weekly average to be slightly lower than this, being 11 crates a week to its pubs. But even so, if all the Carlisle pubs were receiving this latter amount then it still shows a steady demand for bottled beers from Carlisle's pub customers. The column for Draught, shows 216 barrels to the pub over the year 1901 and 217 for 1902.

The price of bottled beer to the customer at the Jovial Sailor at this time was between 2d and 3d a bottle while the price of a draught pint of Mild was 2d and that of Bitter 3d. The bottles though, were not exactly an economical buy as they only contained half a pint,full pint beer bottles for some reason were rarely used by the Carlisle brewers and independent bottlers of the 1894 - 1916 era.

The colours of Victorian glass beer bottles are certainly eye-catching but this was only a minor consideration to the breweries when they originally ordered them from the glass works. There was a preference for opaque bottles like black or dark green glass (rather than clear or white) as brewers considered that beer kept better in bottles made from dark glass. It was known that when clear glass bottled beers were stored in a situation that allowed daylight to play upon them, then after about 10 days the action of the light caused the beer to lose its brightness and go cloudy. Beers in coloured glass bottles could stand in these conditions longer before being affected. In practice though bottled beers were rarely exposed or stored in bright conditions either at the brewery or public house. Even so many brewers remained cautious in this respect and continued to use dark glass bottles.

Another reason and probably the more important of the two, why brewers were disinclined to use clear glass bottles, was the problem of sediment/deposit, the advantage of using a dark coloured glass bottle was obvious if the beer was prone to throwing down an excessive sediment as this unsightly deposit advertised in a clear glass bottle would not have exactly promoted its sale.

If there were some advantages using dark coloured glass bottles there was also one definite disadvantage in that they were difficult to inspect for cleanliness. Most Victorian beer bottles were returned via the publican to the brewery, washed and eventually refilled. When bottling they would have been handling hundreds of bottles, but with the denser coloured types it was impossible to be sure at a quick glance just how clean they were. A part solution was to employ the use of tinted bottles like light green and amber and these were more often used when the beer threw just a slight deposit. It was also felt that the amber bottles in particular retained the light resisting properties (as referred to above).

All Victorian beer bottles, either glass or stoneware, were intended for reuse. They were heavy and in the main well made and as a result were quite durable. There must have been some sort of cash deposit offered so as to enable the breweries to get the bulk of their bottles returned. It is known the Carlisle lemonade firm Underwoods, about 1905, gave a halfpenny on every empty stoneware ginger beer bottle returned. Glass beer bottles being cheaper to produce probably only carried a farthing on each bottle.

Finally some of the names branded or embossed onto the bottles illustrated, were not brewers but bottlers, they were generally wine and spirit merchants and some free-trade publicans who in the main did not bottle Carlisle brewed beer but that of Burton and Irish Stout, in particular from a Dublin brewer known as Findlater.

Above: these bottles were in use c 1902 - 1912. The
address given was the location of the Angel Inn.
Frederick Oberlin Bewsher held the licence from 1887,
but seems not to have displayed the pubs original name
on the property. Instead a board was put up advertising
Bewshers Vaults.

Above: Grahams brewery stocked up with these bottles
circa 1895. Further batches would be ordered from time
to time to make up for bottle loss and they were in use
up to circa 1904.

Considering just how close this brewery was to Carlisle, it is surprising to find that it had hardly any outlets in the city. Only one pub can be traced, this being the spirit vaults in Bell's Court Rickergate, which were retailing the brewery's beer in 1900/01.

George Ismay was a wine and spirit merchant and also publican of the Hare and Hound in Botchergate. The bottle dates to circa 1891. The X sign was commonly used in the 19th century for indicating the strength of beer (the more Xs, the stronger the drink, six Xs being about the limit.).

Above: this stoneware bottle like most of the others shown in this book was made at the pottery of A Buchan, Portobello near Edinburgh. Just above the pottery mark on the rear of the bottle are the figures 07. For some reason this was a digital dating often used by Buchans (post 1903) for giving the manufacturing year. In the case of this bottle, it means it was made in 1907.

Above: this stoneware bottle (date 1911) was used for the retail of lowalcoholic ginger beer, but, as referred to at the start of this book, the Bacchus trademark was frequently used by T and J Minns on their spirit and beer bottles.

Above: despite this bottle being of the earlier cork stoppered and shoulder design it is, in fact, not as old as it
looks. It dates to the years 1912 - 16 when R Lowry was
licensee of the Bricklayers Arms in Caldewgate.

Above: this bottle dates circa 1889. Andrew Patterson
was the licensee of the Golden Lion in Botchergate from
1880 - March 1890. Embossed around the shoulders of
this bottle are the words "Imperial half pint."

Above: James Nasmith took over the grocers and off licence shop at Blackwell Road (see photo page 33) from William Finlay on the 2 February 1903 and remained as tenant up to 1905.

Above: This bottle must have been sold in the Fox and Hounds as 25 Rickergate was the address of the pub. James Clarke was tenant here in 1899 but seemingly not the licence holder. It is difficult to date this bottle accurately, but it is definitely pre 1907.

Above: screw stoppered beer bottle circa 1889. The bottle carries a trade mark of a latticed globe with a V notch cut into it at the one 'o' clock position. This curious badge may be explained by J.W.Hope being related to the Hopes of Kerse whose family heraldry was a shattered /fractured globe. A latin motto also appears on the bottle which roughly translates 'Hope Remains Unbroken'.

Above: screw stoppered Carlisle New Brewery bottle made by Redfearn's glass works in Barnsley circa 1899. Amber glass bottles used by the New Brewery seem to have been for their *Australian Pale Ale, (*retailed in Carlisle) judging by the remains of paper labels which are sometimes still attached to these bottles.

Above: this flask is difficult to date accurately as John Reay was licensee of the Prince of Wales over a long period from 1892 - 1916. Even though the pub's license was held by him it is known that he did not live on the premises. The actual running of the property was carried out by a tenant whom he and the brewery had appointed.

Above: unlike the Reay flask this Star Music Hall bottle can be accurately dated as it was retrieved from an old Carlisle rubbish dump that is known to have been in use between 1891 -1893.

Left: this bottle dates to the years 1905-1907 (see page 92). It is interesting to note that two of the flasks on this page advertise the licensed premises as hotels. Yet there is little evidence to suggest that either of these two properties catered for guests during the years 1894-1916. In fact it is known that by 1905 the first floor of the Black Bull had been converted to a billiard room.

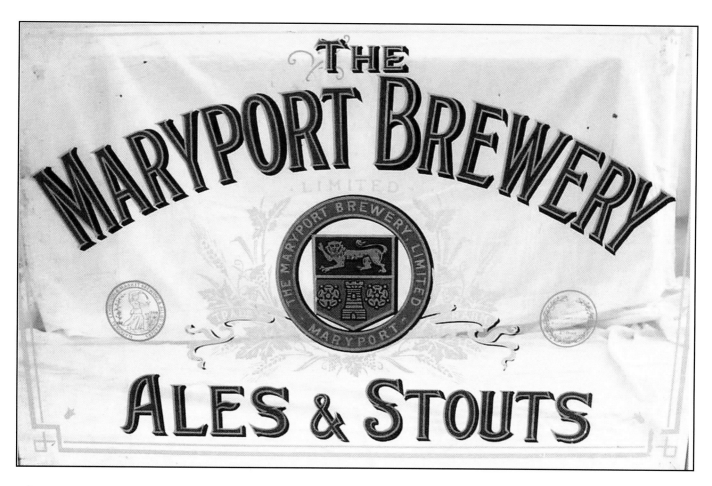

Above: as referred to earlier in this publication the Maryport Brewery had, by the 1890's, a considerable influence on Carlisle's public house trade and so the inclusion of this glass mirror advert is not out of place in a book about the city's pubs in the 1894/1916 era. Of note in the advert are the gold circles left and right of the brewery's lion and turret badge. These are in fact meant to represent the Brewing and Allied Trades Award medal. This was given to firms who entered their beers (and were judged to be of a high standard) at the annual Brewers' Exhibition held in London. In the case of

the above advert we are informed that the brewery had won, in 1905, the 2nd prize in the Class V beer competition. What beer type and gravity 'Class V' is meant to represent though is not made clear. Unfortunately during the course of research for this book it has not been possible to find out whether or not any Carlisle breweries won medals at this exhibition.

Left: this stained glass sign can still be found in situ at the Jovial Sailor in Caldewgate. It is presumably an original fitting that dates to the building of the pub in 1904.